Reforming U.S. Taxes

Albert K. Francisco Ph.D., CPA

reformingustaxes.com

Copyright © 2014 Albert K. Francisco

All rights reserved.

Published by: Accounting Institute Seminars®, Inc.
PO Box 4520
Pocatello, Idaho 83205-4520

Library of Congress Control Number 2014902155

ISBN-13: 978-1494362690

ISBN-10: 1494362694

DEDICATION

To my lovely wife, Maxine Anderson,
who encouraged this project from beginning to end.

CONTENTS

ACKNOWLEDGMENTS	i
1 INTRODUCTION	1
2 IMPORT DUTIES, EXCISE TAXES,	9
PAYROLL TAXES	9
3 PROPERTY TAX and WEALTH TAX	13
4 SALES TAX and the Value Added Tax	17
5 INDIVIDUAL INCOME TAX	21
6 CORPORATE INCOME TAX, ALTERNATIVE MINIMUM TAX	29
7 ESTATE AND GIFT TAX	35
8 HIDDEN TAXES	39
9 CHOOSING AN OPTIMAL TAX STRUCTURE	43
10 CONCLUSION	61
BIBLIOGRAPHY	71
TAX DICTIONARY	77
INDEX	97

ACKNOWLEDGMENTS

Thanks to my business partner Ken Smith of the College of Business at Idaho State University. Many of the ideas in this book were developed with Ken in the process of teaching and writing the many classes we've taught together for people taking the CPA examination.

1 INTRODUCTION

WHY WE HAVE GOVERNMENTS

People sometimes say that private enterprise is preferable to using governments to provide services. Consider using private enterprise instead of a government operated fire department. Would you want to call several fire-fighting companies and ask for bids when you smell smoke in your kitchen? Long ago people found that we need an immediate response to a fire alarm and the community members volunteered or paid in advance for fire fighting service. Today we prepay for fire department and police services as part of our property taxes.

Similarly, our country needs a military to protect the citizens from external threats. Powerful militaries owned and controlled by private companies would be a danger to the citizens since they would have no control over what the military does. The U.S. military is under the control of the civilian government and we pay for it with our federal taxes.

Years ago gasoline contained a lead additive to improve engine performance, but the exhaust was emitted into the air that people breathed. Studies showed that the increased levels of lead in a child's blood lowered intelligence significantly, so the federal Environmental Protection Agency (EPA) outlawed lead additives in gas over time, giving us today's reformulated unleaded gas and a healthier population. [1] The EPA is funded by our federal

---

[1] Philip Shabecoff, "E.P.A. Orders 90 Percent Cut In Lead Content Of Gasoline By 1986", *New York Times*, March 5, 1985

taxes. Private companies act in the best interests of their stockholders and government regulation has been shown to be necessary to place limits on what companies can do.

HOW DO WE PAY FOR PUBLIC SERVICES AND CONTROL SPENDING?

Many taxes are imposed by local, state and federal governments in the U.S. Why are there so many taxes? If you analyze your property tax bill you'll likely find a fire department levy, which goes directly to the fire department and a school levy which goes directly to the school district. Each of these taxes is controlled by the citizens who vote in public elections. Either the voters approve the levy directly in the vote or they elect a city or county legislative body which votes to impose the tax. Citizens have indirect control over the taxes approved by a city council since they can vote for different council members at the next election.

Similarly, spending by the state and federal governments must be authorized by legislative action. We, the voters, control the spending indirectly by being able to vote to change the members of the legislature if we don't like their spending choices.

People who live in local taxing districts benefit directly from services such as police, firefighting, and storm sewers in their districts, so property taxes are levied based on the value of the property. The idea is that someone who owns more (and more valuable) property benefits more from such services than someone in more modest circumstances.

HISTORICAL VIEW OF OBJECTIVES OF TAXATION

Taxes aren't exactly a new subject of discussion. "The art of taxation consists in so plucking the goose as to get the most feathers with the least hissing." [2]

---

[2] attributed to Jean Baptiste Colbert, French economist and minister of finance who lived from 1619 to 1683.

In 1778 Economist Adam Smith, in "The Wealth of Nations" wrote at greater length:

> "... it is necessary to premise the four following maxims with regard to taxes in general.
>
> I. The subjects of every state ought to contribute towards the support of the government, as nearly as possible, in proportion to their respective abilities; that is, in proportion to the revenue which they respectively enjoy under the protection of the state.
>
> II. The tax which each individual is bound to pay ought to be certain, and not arbitrary. The time of payment, the manner of payment, the quantity to be paid, ought all to be clear and plain to the contributor, and to every other person.
>
> III. Every tax ought to be levied at the time, or in the manner, in which it is most likely to be convenient for the contributor to pay it.
>
> IV. Every tax ought to be so contrived as both to take out and to keep out of the pockets of the people as little as possible over and above what it brings into the public treasury of the state. " [3]

EQUITABLE TAXATION

As Adam Smith proposed in his first maxim, one approach to making taxes equitable is to impose taxes so that those who benefit the most pay the most. Some taxes are clearly related to benefit – those who drive more miles on the highways purchase more gasoline or diesel fuel, thus paying more motor fuel tax than those who use the highways less. User fees for water and sewers are paid by those connected to the system. This is known as the benefit principle.

Other taxes have a more indirect relation to the benefit derived from government. More income tax is paid by a person with a higher income. In

---

[3] Adam Smith, "An Inquiry into the Nature and Causes of the Wealth of Nations Vol. II, 2nd edition", (London, W. Strahan and T. Cadell 1778), 425

a sense the higher income individual benefits more from the protection of the legal and economic system administered by government, but it isn't a direct relationship, so this is called the ability to pay principle.

Horizontal equity means people in similar economic circumstances pay similar amounts. Vertical equity means those with higher incomes or greater wealth pay more tax than do those with less. How, though, do you decide how much more the person with greater income or wealth should pay?

INCIDENCE OF TAXATION

Who ends up paying the tax? This is a complex question because many taxes are passed on to others. Import duties are paid by the importer, but are included in the price paid by the eventual purchaser of the goods. Corporate income taxes and property taxes are eventually passed to the buyers of goods produced by those companies, although if the company is unable to raise prices they may result to some extent in lower dividends to shareholders.

PROGRESSIVE VERSUS REGRESSIVE TAXES

Progressive tax rates increase as income increases, while regressive tax rates decrease as income increases. With a proportional tax everyone pays the same percentage of income.

Economists argue that an additional dollar of income to spend is more valuable to someone who earns $10,000 a year than that same dollar is to someone who earns $500,000 a year. Thus, a dollar of additional tax is more painful to the lower earning individual, providing justification for a progressive tax system. Income taxes are generally progressive since those with higher incomes pay a higher percentage of each additional dollar earned than those with lower income pay.

Sales taxes are regressive because people with a lower income are obliged to spend most of their income each year, paying a higher portion of their income on sales taxes than higher income individuals who are able to save or invest a greater percentage. The U.S. does not have a national sales tax; however, states and cities rely heavily on this tax. Tobacco taxes are regressive because those with lower incomes are more likely to smoke and there is a limit to the amount of tobacco one person can consume, so higher income individuals pay a lower percentage of their income on tobacco taxes.

The income tax and estate tax are progressive because the marginal tax rate increases as income or the value of the estate increase. If you are in the 15% bracket you pay 15% of your income. However, if your income is higher and you are in the 39.6% bracket you still pay 15% on the first dollars of your income – only the last few dollars of your income are taxed at 39.6%. This results in an average tax rate somewhere between 15% and 39.6%.

The social security tax on wages is regressive because it applies to only a limited amount of wages ($113,700 in 2013). People who earn more than this limit pay a smaller percentage of their total income as their income increases. It is also regressive because it applies only to wages, not to income from investments and rents. Another criticism is that it taxes wages, thus discouraging people from working. Economists suggest taxing things you want to discourage, like tobacco use, not things you want to encourage, like productive work.

OTHER CRITERIA USED TO CHOOSE A TAX STRUCTURE

Adam Smith's second maxim (that "the tax which each individual is bound to pay ought to be certain") reminds us that it is desirable that a tax system be as simple to understand as possible and not disrupt market forces more than necessary.

Our tax system in the U.S. is clearly not simple and studies show that taxes do affect markets. For example, since capital gains are taxed at a lower rate than ordinary income, people are motivated to find ways to convert ordinary income to capital gains taxed at the lower rate.

A very practical criteria is the government's ability to collect the tax (Adam Smith's third maxim) and the cost of collection. A tax is undesirable if the government is unable to enforce the tax law, or the tax is inefficient because the cost of collection is an unusually large percentage of the tax collected (Adam Smith's fourth maxim).

The total cost of a tax has several parts. One is the administrative system needed to enforce it. Another is the compliance cost on the part of the taxpayer (such as the time to complete required forms). Perhaps the greatest cost is the risk of the adverse effect some taxes can have on economic activity in a society. For example, a tax on earnings set so high that people prefer to spend the day drinking in a bar instead of working would be a terrible drain on the productivity of a society as well as its health.

Another example is our current mishmash of state and local sales taxes, with each requiring its own (expensive) bureaucracy to enforce the tax. Currently businesses that operate under the jurisdiction of many local governments have to understand many varied rules and rates that apply to each locale. These collection costs must be considered in any comparison of tax structures, and our sales tax structure appears to be terribly inefficient in comparison to a uniform system of tax.

Some people work hard to avoid paying tax. The courts have said that structuring ones affairs so as to minimize taxation (tax avoidance) is legal, but tax evasion is illegal and will be punished. [4] One way to evade taxes is to use investment vehicles in countries that obscure the owners of accounts (numbered Swiss bank accounts come to mind), but the IRS periodically discovers such schemes and makes life very uncomfortable for those who use them to evade taxes. The ultimate tax avoidance scheme is to move to another country – but that doesn't work unless one gives up U.S. citizenship, quite a drastic step. The U.S. taxes citizens on income earned anywhere in the world.

The corporate income tax is easy to collect in the U.S. However, unlike individuals, the government taxes U.S. corporations only on their U.S. income, not that earned in other countries. Companies avoid the tax by moving profitable operations to other countries with lower tax rates, in some cases paying almost no U.S. tax. This tax is criticized by economists because a corporation isn't the ultimate recipient of the income which eventually goes to shareholders. Thus, the corporate income is taxed twice, once to the corporation and again to the shareholder who receives dividends. This level of taxation may discourage investment in corporations, diverting it to other investments which may not be the most efficient investments for our economy as a whole.

---

[4] "Over and over again the Courts have said that there is nothing sinister in so arranging affairs as to keep taxes as low as possible." The case of Gregory v. Helvering 69 F.2d 809, 810 (2d Cir. 1934), aff'd, 293 U.S. 465, 55 S.Ct. 266, 79 L.Ed. 596 (1935)

REFORMING U.S. TAXES

Restructuring our tax system so as to nudge people in directions that will improve society, without giving orders or absolute prohibitions, seems to fit with our free enterprise system in the U.S. [5]

OUR CURRENT TAX SYSTEM

In the U.S. today, local governments depend primarily on the property tax, a fixed percentage of the value of property owned. State governments are mainly supported by sales taxes and income taxes. The federal government mostly taxes individual income and wages. In addition to the income tax, wages, salaries, self employment income and other earnings from personal services (like royalties to authors of books) are taxed to support the social security and Medicare systems.

There are many other possible taxes than those that primarily fund our public services today. Other countries use a wider variety of taxes such as import duties, wealth taxes, and the VAT (Value Added Tax). In the following pages we will explore how our current tax system is structured and consider some alternatives.

POSSIBILITY OF CHANGING THE SYSTEM

Many people are dissatisfied with our current tax system. The current Congress seems reluctant to agree on anything, and yet that dissatisfaction is evident on both the left and the right. The last major change was made in 1986. Proposals have been made to start with an estimate of the necessary federal revenue, then assume no deductions, exemptions, credits, or other breaks for particular taxpayers, which could lead to surprisingly low tax rates. From there, each proposed reduction in tax for particular groups would have to be justified with the knowledge that the rest of the taxpayers would face higher rates if that provision becomes part of the law. [6]

---

[5] The book *Nudge,* by Thaler and Sunstein, describes the economics of nudging people in directions that produce greater overall happiness.
[6] Floyd Norris," Economy: Window Is Opening For Change In Tax Code,"
New York Times, Jan. 16, 2014

Albert K. Francisco

ENFORCEMENT OF TAX LAWS

Politicians find criticizing the IRS and state tax agencies to be popular among voters, so they seldom mention enforcement of the tax laws except to criticize the tax police. But those tax agencies are collecting money that will be used to finance public services on which we all rely. If people evade their tax obligations that increases the amounts the rest of us have to pay, increases the public debt, or results in fewer government services. Voters always seem to prefer taxes that someone else will pay, but we all benefit from the structure of our society in the U.S. and we should be pleased that those who lived before us created such a successful system for us to enjoy today. If tax evasion grows over time future generations will not find life so pleasant.

The tax gap is the percentage of the tax due that is not collected for various reasons. This varies with different kinds of taxes and should be considered in choosing the optimal tax structure.

USING THIS BOOK

Tax specialists have their own language which is sometimes quite different from ordinary English. Their words have precise meanings (to them!). You may be familiar with some terms, but not with others. You might mark the DICTIONARY on page 77 so you can refer to it when necessary.

This book is based on tax laws in effect for the 2013 calendar year. As you are undoubtedly aware, many tax provisions change each year and tax laws for future years may be quite different. This book is intended to be an overview of general tax concepts. It does not present advice on specific tax situations. Consult a competent CPA for advice relevant to your own situation.

2 IMPORT DUTIES, EXCISE TAXES, PAYROLL TAXES

Customs duties are imposed when goods are imported from other countries Excise taxes are also imposed on goods produced within a country. The U.S. imposes excise taxes on the sale of gasoline and diesel fuel, generally using the tax to pay for highway construction or repair with the rationale that users pay to support the highways.

SIN TAXES

Taxes can be used to discourage the use of specific products. Sin taxes are excise taxes imposed on products that have demonstrated harmful effects, such as tobacco, which causes cancer, and alcohol which may lead to alcoholism. The U.S. imposes significant excise taxes on alcohol and tobacco. This discourages their purchase, leading to fewer harmful effects on the population.

Worldwide alcohol related deaths have increased rapidly in recent years, from 750,000 in 1990 to 2,500,000 in 2011. The least expensive alcoholic drinks have been shown to cause the most ill-health and early deaths. Some jurisdictions are moving to tax those enough to discourage usage and that has been shown to significantly improve the health of the population. British Columbia in Canada instituted a minimum price for a drink (which increases as the percent of alcohol increases) in 2002. The price increase, an average of only 10%, resulted in a 32% decline in deaths caused solely by alcohol between 2002 and 2009. [7] A tax on alcohol content high enough to reduce the consumption of inexpensive drinks would improve health and cut costs of alcohol related accidents in the U.S.

The country of Uruguay[8] and the U.S. states of Colorado and Washington[9] recently legalized the sale of recreational marijuana, but are planning to tax it heavily.

Mexico recently instituted a tax on sodas and high calorie foods because of the heavy burden obesity and diabetes places on their national health system.[10] Companies who profit from junk food and soda sales have contributed heavily to oppose such taxes when they've been proposed in U.S. cities.

These taxes are becoming more important to the U.S. economy as the costs of health care rise. According to The Economist "by the early 2020s the taxpayer will be footing the bill for half of America's health spending" (through Medicare, Medicaid, and health care for the government's own employees).[11] Thus, to limit increases in taxes it is important to nudge people in the direction of healthier lifestyles. Not everyone will welcome these sin taxes, but taxpayers overall will have reason to rejoice if they are instituted and are effective.

Another potential excise tax that can be viewed as a sin tax is one on agricultural fertilizers. Water from the Mississippi River, rich in crop fertilizer from farm fields upstream, flows into the Gulf of Mexico, creating a dead

---

[7] "Mulled Whines – Alcohol Pricing", *The Economist*, Dec. 21, 2013, 99.

[8] Simon Romero, "Uruguay Acts to Legalize Marijuana", New York Times, December 10, 2013

[9] Dan Frosch, "Measures To Legalize Marijuana Are Passed", New York Times, November 6, 2013

[10] Paulina Villega, "Mexico: Junk Food Tax Is Approved," *New York Times*, October 31, 2013

[11] "Going public, and private – Health care in America", *The Economist*, December 21, 2013.

zone that now spans 6,700 square miles. It is estimated to cost fisheries $2.8 billion each year. [12]

IMPORT DUTIES (CUSTOMS TARIFFS)

Early in the history of the U.S. customs import duties were an important source of government revenue. In addition, by increasing the cost of products from other countries the U.S. was able to protect and encourage domestic production. These duties were imposed at different rates on different products.

Economic theory eventually found, however, that lowering duties imposed on purchases from other countries encouraged production in the most efficient country, making more goods available overall to be shared between the various countries. This led to a lowering of customs duties, and even their elimination in free trade areas such as NAFTA, the North American Free Trade Agreement.

Domestic industries periodically demand protection from foreign competition however, so duties are sometimes imposed or increased to protect domestic employment or to penalize another country for "dumping" – exporting goods at a price less than their cost of production to keep their own citizens employed.

A similar approach is to impose import bans or quotas, so limiting the quantity of a foreign good that can be imported. The reduced supply results in a higher price, protecting domestic production. Like import duties, economists say these quotas result in suboptimal production for the world as a whole and a decrease in worldwide income.

PAYROLL TAXES

The U.S. relies primarily on payroll taxes to finance social security (FICA) and Medicare benefits for the elderly and disabled. The social security tax is

---

[12] Lisa Palmer, "Green - Floating Islands to the Rescue", *New York Times*, February 15, 2013

regressive because it applies only to the first $113,700 of earned income. Those with higher income and those who have income from investments don't pay the social security tax on that income.

Economists believe that the ultimate impact of these payroll taxes is to reduce the wages that would otherwise be paid.[13] If the country could find an alternative way to finance the social security and Medicare systems that isn't so regressive it would improve the perceived vertical equity of our tax system.

On the other hand, social security benefits to retired people are quite progressive, so the combination of the tax and benefits means the social security program overall is not regressive. [14] And taxpayers view their social security and Medicare benefits as earned by their payments of those taxes, so don't mind paying them as much as they otherwise might. This is a powerful argument for continuing to fund them with these payroll taxes instead of replacing the payroll taxes with a less regressive tax.

---

[13] Leonard E. Burman and Joel Slemrod, *Taxes in America*, (New York, Oxford University Press, 2013), 32.
[14] Burman and Slemrod, 52.

3 PROPERTY TAX and WEALTH TAX

A property tax is a fixed percentage of the value of property owned. Without this tax people would be more likely to hold real estate hoping for gain, keeping it from uses helpful to society. Imposing an annual property tax encourages the owners to put the land to productive use or to sell it to someone who will put it to use.

Some criticize property taxes as unfair to lower income retired persons trying to stay in their own homes. This problem has been addressed in some jurisdictions by reductions or exemptions from the tax on owner-occupied homes given to those with lower incomes. City and county governments in the U.S. rely heavily on property tax although taxpayers in some have placed limits that restrict annual increases, such as not allowing the increase each year to be more than the general inflation rate.

Cities have higher property tax rates than surrounding areas. This encourages people and companies to move planned construction out to the suburbs, decreasing population density and resulting in inefficiencies because of the additional costs of providing services such as water, sewers, and public transit to widely separated buildings. Financing city services with property taxes and sales taxes can lead to boom and bust cycles; a city with declining population sees both its property tax receipts decrease (because of lower property values) and its sales tax receipts decrease because of fewer purchases by a smaller and poorer population.

In 1978 California enacted Proposition 13 through a statewide referendum, bringing in the era of limits on taxation. [15] Proposition 13 limited increases in property tax to 2% per year, putting many taxing districts under considerable strain since the population expected increased public services but the law didn't allow property tax increases to fund those services. [16] This has resulted in great inequity because the property tax on newly purchased property is based on the sales price, while identical property that has been owned for many years is valued at a much lower amount. The state has tried to find alternative taxes and fees to make up the lost revenue, without great success. Revaluing property annually for property tax purposes clearly produces a higher level of horizontal equity, but in a democracy such considerations don't override the will of the voters. One alternative is a higher consumption tax combined with increased levies on estates and gifts. However, this moves away from the concept of tying the tax to the benefit, and the value of property is clearly related to the benefit of fire and police protection for that property.

STATE AND LOCAL PENSIONS

State and local governments are generally required to balance their budgets each year. There is one glaring exception to that rule, and it is the pension they've agreed to pay their employees after retirement. State and local legislative bodies find it convenient to spend money on current benefits for taxpayers, but difficult to set aside funds to make pension payments that have been promised to public employees after retirement. As a result, many state and local governments are woefully short of funds to cover those promises. Unfortunately, their employees often aren't covered by the social security system, so retirees won't have that system as a backstop to their local government pensions.

The Governmental Accounting Standards Board (GASB), passes rules that govern the preparation of state and local financial statements. One of their rules specifies the required annual contribution needed for a pension fund to eventually meet obligations that have been incurred. [17] But there is no legal

---

[15] See Wikipedia page "California Proposition 13"
[16] Rob Reich, "Not Very Giving", *New York Times*, September 4, 2013
[17] Governmental Accounting Standards Board Statement 25, "Financial Reporting for Defined Benefit Pension Plans and Note Disclosures for Defined Contribution Plans", Norwalk, CT, November 1994

requirement that governments actually set aside that money, just a rule in the GASB rulebook. So many governments look the other way and underfund their pension plans year after year. The result is that either pension promises of state and local governments won't be kept or future taxpayers will be asked to cough up extra money to make up for what taxpayers in prior years failed to provide.

WEALTH TAXES

A wealth tax is a percentage of the value of everything a person owns (often reduced by debts owed). It is sometimes imposed on only the value of intangible assets, such as stocks and bonds. It is justified as equitable since wealth is a clear measure of ability to pay. France and Spain currently have individual wealth taxes., but only Switzerland raises significant revenue from this type of tax. [18] Annual wealth taxes are supported by arguments that they decrease inequality and improve a country's vertical equity. There is a difficulty in property valuation, since it changes from year to year and may not have been measured by a sale for many years. Also, highly valuable assets that aren't large (such as jewelry and some art) are difficult for taxing authorities to detect and offer opportunities to evade the tax for those so inclined.

In a sense property taxes are wealth taxes, but are imposed on the total value of property, not reduced by mortgage debt.

Estate and gift taxes are a different form of wealth tax, imposed on the transfer of assets at death (estate tax) and between living individuals (gift tax).

---

[18] Eurostat Statistical Books, "Taxation trends in the European Union", 2013.

4 SALES TAX and the Value Added Tax

Most states impose a sales tax, but five do not. Alaska, Delaware, Montana, New Hampshire and Oregon have no sales tax. Since Washington state has no income tax and Oregon no sales tax, people who live and work in Vancouver, WA, just across the Columbia River from Portland, OR, pay no income tax and find it convenient to shop in Portland, with no sales tax. This seems to be an unfair advantage over other U.S. citizens, leading to horizontal inequity. New Hampshire has significantly lower alcohol and tobacco taxes than most other states, and locates their state liquor stores conveniently near the major highways entering the state. Making taxes uniform across the country would address these inequalities.

States compete to offer incentives to businesses that locate there. When these incentives take the form of reduced taxes they increase the relative tax burden on other taxpayers. Since most states are active in this competition the benefit to one state is offset with a cost to other states, resulting in a zero sum game. There doesn't seem to be a way to stop this competition to reduce taxes other than to impose a uniform tax system to raise state revenue nationwide.

General sales taxes apply to sales of most products. Some states exempt some products, such as groceries and medicines. This makes it less of a burden for lower income consumers who spend a greater percentage of their income on food and medicine than higher income individuals. Rates vary greatly across the country, with many cities adding to the state sales tax for sales within the city. This results in people paying much different levels of tax on identical purchases in different jurisdictions, an insult to horizontal equity.

States are not allowed by the federal constitution to impose state taxes on interstate commerce, so they can't collect sales tax on sales to their residents by companies in other states. Generally a use tax (the sales tax is collected for using an out of state purchase in the state) is imposed by states with sales taxes to collect the tax on sales to their residents by out-of-state companies. There has been considerable litigation since out-of-state companies with no facilities within a state often don't wish to collect the tax for the myriad governments (state, county, city) in that state.

Currently the law generally requires that a company have a physical presence (nexus) in a state for the state to require collection of the tax, but the meaning of nexus is unclear. Does it require that the company own a physical structure, or just pay sales agents in the state? Is mailing advertising material to residents of a state sufficient to allow the state to require collection of the tax? [19] Replacing the many varied rules of the state and local governments with one uniform law nationwide, perhaps allowing the state and local governments to set their own rates within that law, would reduce the costs of compliance, enforcement and litigation greatly.

Value added taxes (VAT) are a variation used in all member countries of the Organization for Economic Co-operation except the USA. The VAT must have significant benefits for so many countries to have adopted it since 1967, when it first appeared in Denmark. [20] Value added taxes differ from sales taxes because the VAT is imposed at each level of production and applies only to the value added at that level of production. A manufacturer pays the tax on its sales to retailers, but receives a credit for the VAT paid by the suppliers of its raw materials. Similarly, the retailer pays the tax on its sales revenue, but claims a credit for the tax paid by its suppliers. The result is that the consumer pays the full amount of the VAT, but it is collected in small amounts from each step along the chain of production, reducing the incentive to evade the tax at each level. Each payer of the tax wants proof that the tax has been paid by its suppliers since that proof allows them to deduct the previously paid tax from what they would otherwise owe on their own sales.

---

[19] Saul Hansell, "New York State Girds for War With Amazon," *New York Times*, APRIL 14, 2008
[20] For a detailed discussion of the history of the VAT and the differences between the VAT and sales taxes see Cedric Sandford, *Why Tax Systems Differ*, (Fiscal Publications, Bath, England, 2000), 75-93

Countries generally refund the VAT paid on products that are exported so as to not make products of their country uncompetitive with those of other countries. They, of course, charge the VAT on imports so they bear the same tax as domestically produced goods.

The VAT is supported by many economists who argue that it is better to tax consumption instead of labor, encouraging both saving and work by not taxing either. It also is an efficient tax, with low costs of collection, and is a potential major source of revenue to address shortages of funds needed to invest in education and infrastructure and to pay escalating social security and Medicare costs as the elderly population inexorably increases due to better health care and longer life spans. [21]

Consumption taxes (sales taxes and value added taxes) are criticized as being regressive, because studies show they take a higher percentage of the income of those who earn the least. People with the highest incomes spend a smaller percentage of their income each year, so pay a smaller percentage of their income on consumption taxes. That criticism can be addressed by periodic refunds of the estimated tax paid by the poor on basic purchases such as groceries.

---

[21] Catherine Rampell, "Value-Added Taxes: A Primer", *New York Times*, April 19, 2010

5 INDIVIDUAL INCOME TAX

The individual income tax adheres closely to Adam Smith's tax goals listed in chapter 1:

I. The income tax is in proportion to the revenue which the citizens respectively enjoy under the protection of the state. The income tax meets the goal of vertical equity since more income means more tax. The current income tax is less successful in meeting the goal of horizontal equity since two taxpayers with the same income, but of types taxed at different rates, will not pay the same tax.

II. The income tax owed by each individual is based on income, which is certain, and not arbitrary. Income tax laws are reasonably consistent from year to year, minimizing unpleasant surprises when taxes are due.

III. Every tax ought to be levied at the time, or in the manner, in which it is most likely to be convenient for the contributor to pay it. Withholding at the source allows the income tax to meet this goal.

IV. Every tax ought to be so contrived as both to take out and to keep out of the pockets of the people as little as possible over and above what it brings into the public treasury of the state. Income taxes have been shown to be efficient when costs of compliance and administration are compared with the funds raised for public purposes.

Most states in the U.S. have an individual income tax at the state level which is based on the federal income tax. This makes the state income tax especially efficient since the costs of administration and compliance are largely already incurred in the federal income tax, so the state taxes add only small marginal costs. Most state taxes paid are deductible in computing federal taxable income, which reduces the burden of taxing the same income twice. Studies have shown that the income tax is viewed as the most fair of the common taxes. [22]

United States tax law follows the accretion concept in defining income (many countries follow other concepts). The accretion concept includes in income any realized increase in wealth, being most clearly articulated in a 1955 Supreme Court decision.[23] A realized increase in wealth usually means the increase in value has been received in cash after selling the asset. The U.S. tax law is global in nature, since it applies to all realized increases in wealth (including capital gains), not just specific categories of income. It differs from tax law in many other countries in that U.S. citizens are taxed on their income from anywhere in the world, not just in the U.S. This sounds like it would result in double taxation of income earned in other countries, but the U.S. allows a credit against the U.S. tax for tax paid on the same income in the other country.

Several items are subtracted from income before an individual's income tax is computed. Exclusions are not included in the definition of gross income. Deductions are either deductions <u>to arrive at</u> AGI or deductions <u>from</u> AGI (adjusted gross income).

Some limits are based on the adjusted gross figure (such as medical deductions). Deductions to arrive at AGI are allowed even if the taxpayer elects the standard deduction. Itemized deductions are allowed only if the standard deduction is not taken.

An individual income tax return follows this order:
    Gross Income
    Less: Deductions to arrive at AGI (incurred in producing income)
    Equals: Adjusted Gross Income (AGI)
    Less: Itemized Deductions or Standard Deduction
    Less: Personal and Dependency Exemptions
    Equals: Taxable Income

---

[22] David Brunori, *The Future of State Taxation*, (The Urban Press, Washington, D.C., 1998), 198
[23] Victor Thuronyi, *Comparative Tax Law*, (Kluwer Law International, The Hague, The Netherlands, 2003), 233, 235

Tax computation
Less: Credits and payments
Equals: Tax payable or refundable

WHAT IS INCLUDED IN GROSS INCOME?

Gross income includes any value received that benefits the recipient. Gifts, some scholarships, and returns of capital already owned are excluded.

Scholarship or fellowship grants paid to a degree candidate by a tax exempt educational organization are excludable by the recipient up to the amount used for books, supplies, and tuition.

Interest earned on public purpose municipal and state obligations is not taxed. There are two types of savings accounts on which earnings can be withdrawn as tax exempt income. Contributions to these plans are not deductible. These are Educational Savings Accounts and Roth IRAs.

Capital gains are gains on the sale of capital assets (nonbusiness property and investments). If a net capital loss occurs in one year, it is subtracted from ordinary income up to a maximum of $3,000. The remaining unused loss is carried forward to the next year. If the asset was held over one year the gain is taxed at a maximum rate of 20%. Similarly, dividends from C corporations are taxed at a maximum of 20%.

Life insurance proceeds are excluded. The beneficiary does not include a life insurance policy payment in gross income if it is due to death of the insured.

Social security benefits are partially taxed to higher income individuals (a maximum of 85% is included in gross income). Welfare benefits are not taxed, but unemployment benefits from a federal or state agency are included in income.

Forgiveness of debt is taxed because the taxpayer has received value. The amount is excluded if the forgiveness was a gift. Bankruptcy relief is excluded.

Excluded fringe benefits include expense allowances, adoption expenses, medical insurance, long-term care insurance, life insurance, education assistance, and benefits with little cost to the employer.

Tax deferred employer payments to a retirement plan (contributions) are not income to the employee until benefits are paid to the employee after retirement. Voluntary employee contributions are tax deferred until retirement. Income earned by pension investments is tax deferred. Withdrawals from pension plans by employees are taxed as ordinary income.

THE STANDARD DEDUCTION

After AGI is found, the taxpayer can itemize deductions from adjusted gross or take the standard deduction. Deductions to arrive at AGI can be taken whether the taxpayer selects the standard deduction or itemized deductions.

The standard deduction is:

Married (joint)	$12,200
Single	$6,100

Extra standard deduction amounts ($1,500 if single and $1,200 if married) are allowed for each taxpayer who is either 65 or older or who is blind.

ITEMIZED DEDUCTIONS

Total itemized deductions are reduced by 3% of AGI over a threshold amount ($300,000 if joint, $250,000 if single).

MEDICAL EXPENSES

Qualifying medical expenses are paid for the taxpayer, spouse, or dependent. Only medical expenses above 10% of AGI are included in total itemized deductions.

TAXES

Federal taxes are not deductible. Deductible taxes include state and local income tax, real property tax and personal property tax.

CONTRIBUTIONS

To be deductible, contributions must be to one of the following (contributions to an individual are not deductible).

1. State, federal or local government in the U.S.
2. Organizations for religious, charitable, scientific, testing for public safety, literary, educational, national/international sports competition, prevention of cruelty to children or animals, volunteer fire and civil defense purposes.
3. Fraternal lodges if the contribution is for a purpose listed in item 2 above.
4. Not-for-profit veteran organizations and cemetery corporations.

INTEREST

Interest on mortgages secured by a principal residence or second residence of up to $1,000,000 principal plus home equity loans up to $100,000 principal can be deducted. Other consumer interest paid is not deductible.

CASUALTY AND THEFT LOSSES

Casualty or theft losses of nonbusiness property above insurance reimbursement are deductible above 10% of AGI. A casualty is an identifiable event that results in a sudden, unexpected or unusual loss. Losses due to gradual decay cannot be deducted.

EXEMPTIONS

A taxpayer is allowed to deduct a personal exemption of $3,900 from AGI for the taxpayer (and the taxpayer's spouse if it is a joint return). In addition, a taxpayer can deduct the same $3,900 for each dependent. The taxpayer must provide over half of the dependent's support. Exemptions are reduced by 2% for each $2,500 of AGI above $300,000 on a joint return and $250,000 on a single return.

Including personal and dependency exemptions in the income tax structure as a deduction is inherently regressive. A $3,900 exemption saves $390 of income tax for a taxpayer in the 10% tax bracket, but $1,544 of tax for someone in the top 39.6% bracket. Why should a personal exemption be worth $1,154 more in real cash money to a high income individual than a low income individual?

Giving the taxpayer a cash credit against the tax for the exemption would mean that the high income and the low income taxpayers would each receive the same cash benefit. That would seem to fit the idea of vertical equity much better than the current regressive system.

TAX CALCULATIONS

In addition to the regular income tax, investment income of individuals, estates and trusts is taxed at 3.8% for those taxpayers who have AGI above $200,000 for single individuals and $250,000 for joint returns. This tax is called the unearned income Medicare contribution tax.

Dividends from C-type corporations and long term capital gains are taxed at 15% (20% for individuals in the top 39.6% bracket).

A refundable earned income credit is available to taxpayers with an adjusted gross income (AGI) below a certain level, The amount varies depending on the number of qualifying children and AGI. The maximum credit for taxpayers with one qualifying child is $3,250, for two children $5,372, and for three children it is $6,044.

OPPORTUNITIES FOR TAX EVASION

The individual income tax is enforced in the U.S. for wages and salaries by requiring employers to withhold the estimated tax due on the compensation and paying it to the government. This greatly reduces the opportunity for the employee to evade the tax. Income on investments, such as dividends and interest, is not subject to withholding, but payers are required to report the amount of income to the government, allowing the tax authorities to match the income reported with that reported by the payer.

The most difficult types of income on which to enforce collection of the tax is income where there is no withholding of the tax at the source and no available documents reporting the income that the tax authorities can match.

Thus it is more expensive for the tax authorities to collect tax on such income than on income subject to withholding or reporting at the source.

This leads to questions of tax equity, if a significant number of taxpayers successfully evade payment of the tax, while very few can evade payment of tax on other sources of income. This is an argument for lower rates of income tax, reducing the tax inequity between taxpayers with various sources of income.

6 CORPORATE INCOME TAX, ALTERNATIVE MINIMUM TAX

People often misunderstand who really pays taxes that are levied on businesses. There is no such thing as a business bearing the burden of taxation – instead the tax will be passed on to real people in the form of lower wages to employees and suppliers, higher prices to consumers, and lower returns to business owners. Taxing a business may be an efficient way of collecting a tax, but the ultimate burden is born by real humans, not a business organization that has been created in the minds of humans but which has no physical existence in itself.

The justification for taxing businesses should be equity of taxation, increased efficiency, and charging for externalities that are caused by business operations – such as ill-health due to pollution emitted by a business. Many activities cause costs to be born by others, such as global warming due to carbon emissions. Taxing businesses at the source of the emissions might be the most efficient and effective way of assuring that the consumers of the business's products and services will ultimately bear the cost.

Also, corporations, like real humans, benefit from government services such as a stable legal system that enforces contracts entered into by the business, public roads, fire and police departments, and schools that educate workers employed by the corporation in the future. An effective way to assure that the ultimate consumers of the company's goods and services pay the cost of those government services is to tax the company for the value of those services.

THE CORPORATE INCOME TAX

Corporations that pay the corporate income tax are known as C-type corporations. Income from partnerships and S-type corporations is taxed to the individual owner only, not also to the business entity.

C-type corporations find taxable income by subtracting deductions from income. The rules differ from individual tax rules in a number of ways. For example, AGI does not apply to corporations.

The tax rates range up to 35%. Certain deductions are not allowed. A corporation has no itemized deductions or standard deduction. There is no personal exemption.

Deductible business expenses include some deductions for amounts never paid by the corporation. Depletion expense is similar to depreciation, but is a deduction of the cost of mineral property. An alternative to deducting its actual cost is known as "percentage depletion" where the expense is computed by multiplying a percentage (which varies depending on the type of mineral) times the income from the property.

Strangely enough, the expense over several years is not limited to the cost of the property. A business can continue to deduct the depletion expense even though the entire cost of the property has already been expensed. This feature of the tax law appears very unfair to other taxpayers who are allowed to deduct expenses only for amounts actually spent.

Gains and losses on transactions involving the corporation's own stock are not taxed. Capital gains and losses are taxed differently than those of individuals. Net capital gains are taxed at the corporation's regular tax rate. Net capital losses cannot be deducted against ordinary income.

U.S. citizens are taxed on their income no matter where in the world it is earned. A corporation, on the other hand, is not taxed on the income from foreign subsidiaries until it is remitted to the U.S. This allows many large corporations to permanently avoid U.S. income tax by moving their most profitable operations to other countries that have low income tax rates, encouraging them to invest in other countries instead of in the U.S.

STOCK REPURCHASES

Some very profitable corporations that have accumulated large amounts of cash are now buying back their own shares instead of paying cash dividends.

Corporate executives really like share buyback plans because many have stock options or bonuses tied to the price per share. When the corporation buys back shares it decreases the number of shares outstanding, leading to an increased price per share. The value of the bonus or stock option is increased through no effort on the part of the executive.

Stockholders often like corporate share buyback plans because they can continue to hold shares that have increased in value (paying no income tax currently), and choose when to sell, or to donate them for an income tax deduction, or to leave them to heirs in their estate.

These last two alternatives allow the income tax to be avoided permanently. The gain isn't taxed when appreciated shares are donated to a charity, and the fair value can be claimed as an itemized deduction. Heirs receive a "stepped-up" basis, meaning the deceased never paid income tax on the gain, the estate never paid income tax on the gain, and the heir never pays income tax on the gain.

CORPORATE EXECUTIVE STOCK OPTIONS

Often the majority of the income of corporate executives comes in the form of stock options, the right to purchase the company's stock at a set price. The value of such options isn't taxed until the stock itself is sold, often many years in the future.

If the stock is held for 12 months after the option is exercised the gain is a long term capital gain taxed at favorable rates. Or, of course, the stock can be donated to a charity, creating a deduction for its fair market value against ordinary income, or held until death when it is included in the estate. That allows the heir to use a stepped-up basis so that nobody is ever taxed on the increase in value.

These options increase in value when current business expenses are reduced. This is an incentive for executives to focus on the near-term and reduce investments in research, advertising, and physical plant. Eliminating the tax benefits for executive stock options would encourage them to take the long view, improving the productive capability of our entire economy.

IMPROVING STATE CORPORATE INCOME TAXES

Most states have a corporate income tax, each with different rules. That complicates the problem of computing the tax for companies that operate in several states and provides an easy way for them to reduce their tax payments by directing income (such as royalties for use of intangible property) to states with low tax rates or no corporate income tax.

If the federal government required states that have an income tax to simply add their tax onto the federal corporate return these problems could be greatly reduced and the costs of administering the tax law and complying with the law reduced as well.

ELIMINATING THE CORPORATE INCOME TAX

Some economists argue persuasively that the corporate income tax should be eliminated. They claim that many U.S. corporations are already successfully avoiding it by moving income to other countries that have low (or zero) corporate tax rates. They say that eliminating the tax would result in those companies moving their investments back to the U.S. which would greatly increase investment and job growth in the U.S. [24]

They also claim that any government revenue loss could be more than offset by increasing the individual income tax rate on corporate dividends and capital gains from selling corporate stock. This does make sense since it is the owners, suppliers, and employees of corporations who ultimately bear the burden of the corporate income tax. The corporation, as a fictitious legal

---

[24] Laurence J. Kotlikoff, "Abolish the Corporate Income Tax," *New York Times*, January 5, 2014

entity, simply passes the tax on to real people by incremental changes in dividends, wages, and prices paid to suppliers.

On the other hand, many nonprofits (organizations exempt from the income tax) have large endowments invested in corporate stock. The corporate income tax paid by the corporation reduces the cash available for distribution as dividends, indirectly taxing the nonprofits. This does provide a way for nonprofits to support the government with a part of the income that would otherwise be earnings accruing to them.

THE ALTERNATIVE MINIMUM TAX (AMT)

Members of Congress must keep the interests of their voters at home in mind. A senator from Texas who votes against the oil and gas depletion allowance (income tax reduction) for income from oil and gas wells would be hounded out of office at the next election (if not before). Senators from Washington and Oregon who voted against the timber depletion allowance would suffer the same fate. And senators from Kentucky and West Virginia who voted against the coal depletion allowance might find they are unwelcome when talking to voters at home. So we don't seem to be able to eliminate these tax benefits for specific types of income.

To offset this, corporations and individuals are supposed to pay an alternative minimum tax if the regular income tax is especially low due to these tax breaks. This is intended to impose a minimum tax rate on all taxpayers, which sounds like a reasonable idea.

However, it doesn't work like that in practice. With competent tax advisors wealthy individuals and corporations can have large amounts of income and pay no AMT.

To find the AMT, start with the regular taxable income and increase it by tax preferences, reduce it by a minimum tax exemption, then multiply the result (alternative minimum taxable income) by the minimum tax rate. The taxpayer then pays the HIGHER of the regular income tax or the alternative minimum tax. So the secret to avoiding the minimum tax is to know what doesn't count as a tax preference.

You've probably heard that interest income on state and local government bonds is exempt from the federal income tax. That surely sounds like a tax preference, but tax exempt interest is NOT included in tax preferences, so doesn't increase the alternative minimum tax. Also, long term capital gains and corporate dividends are taxed at a maximum 20% rate, which sounds like quite a good deal compared to the 39.6% maximum tax rate on ordinary income. But corporate dividends and long term capital gains aren't included in tax preferences, even though they are clearly taxed at a preferential rate.

The alternative minimum tax was intended to stop wealthy taxpayers from avoiding the income tax, but today it is mostly paid by middle income taxpayers, not the rich. The rich can afford tax advisors who can tell them how to avoid this extremely complicated tax, and their political influence make it unlikely the AMT will be reformed so they actually pay it. The AMT raises a lot of revenue, so it would be difficult for Congress to repeal it.[25]

If you are happy with a general discussion of the AMT you can skip the rest of the gory details in this chapter. The alternative minimum tax applies to individuals, larger corporations, estates and trusts. Alternative minimum taxable income (AMTI) is regular taxable income plus tax preferences less an AMT exemption.

The AMT exemption is $40,000 for corporations, $80,800 on joint returns, and $51,900 on single returns. Multiply the AMTI by the alternative minimum tax rate to find the tentative alternative minimum tax. For individuals, the rate is 26% up to $175,000 and 28% above that. For corporations, the rate is 20%.

The tentative AMT is compared with the regular income tax. If the tentative AMT is larger, the regular income tax is paid plus AMT equal to the difference between the regular tax and the tentative AMT. Thus, the total tax paid equals the tentative AMT.

---

[25] Leonard E. Burman and Joel Slemrod, *Taxes in America*, (New York, Oxford University Press, 2013), 44.

7 ESTATE AND GIFT TAX

The U.S. tax system includes an estate and gift tax. This tax is sometime described as a death tax, but that is incorrect because it isn't imposed on every death. Instead, it is imposed only on the fair value of the estates (property owned) of wealthy people. Wealthy in this case means the person had net assets (assets less liabilities) above $5,250,000 ($10,500,000 for married couples). An inheritance tax is similar, but is paid by the heir who inherits the property. The estate tax is paid by the executor of the estate from the assets of the estate, so the U.S. doesn't have an inheritance tax.

Estates could escape the estate tax entirely if the person gave away the property while they were alive. To stop this method of avoiding the tax, the same tax is imposed on gifts between living people. The entire system is called the unified estate and gift tax or unified transfer tax.

Transfer taxes are levied on transfers of property when equal value is not received in return. If the transferor is alive when control is relinquished, the gift tax applies. If the transfer occurs because of death, estate tax applies. If property transfers to individuals one or more generations beyond the deceased, the generation-skipping tax may also apply.

GIFT TAX

Gifts are valued at fair market value at the date of gift. The gift tax uses the estate tax rates. Each donor has a lifetime gift tax credit that can be deducted from gift tax on a cumulative basis until the lifetime credit is consumed. The applicable credit eliminates gift tax on taxable gifts of $5,250,000 ($10,500,000 for a married couple) over a lifetime.

Also the first $14,000 of value from one taxpayer to another in each tax year is exempt from gift tax (the annual exclusion). A married couple can elect to split gifts and thereby exempt $28,000 to the same donee (even if all of the gift was from one spouse). There is no limit on the number of exempt donees.

Gifts in any amount to qualified charities are excluded. Gifts to a spouse are not subject to gift tax (there is an unlimited marital deduction). Transfers to political organizations are excluded. Property settlements incident to divorce are excluded.

Qualified payments of medical expenses or tuition made on behalf of another person <u>directly</u> to the medical care provider or educational institution are excluded, as are support payments required by state law.

Gift tax is calculated by accumulating all taxable gifts from that donor during his or her lifetime, computing the tax on total gifts, and subtracting gift tax paid in prior years. Gifts are taxed at marginal rates on a cumulative basis at the same rates used for the estate tax.

ESTATE TAX

The gross estate includes all property over which control or enjoyment ceases at death. Property is valued for the estate at fair market value on the date of death.

Some items can be deducted (without limit) from the gross estate to find the taxable estate. These deductions include casualty or theft losses, liabilities outstanding at death, funeral and administration costs, the unlimited marital deduction for property transferred to the surviving spouse, and charitable contributions authorized by the will.

Estate tax is calculated the same way as gift tax. Lifetime taxable gifts are added to the taxable estate and the estate tax is calculated at marginal rates that range from 18% to a maximum of 40%. (Marginal rates mean that the 40% rate applies only to estate value above the beginning of that rate bracket.) Prior gift tax paid and other credits are subtracted. And, of course, no estate tax is due if the value of the estate is below $5,250,000 ($10,500,000 for a married couple).

Estate tax credits include the applicable credit, which eliminates estate tax on the first $5,250,000 of estate value ($10,500,000 for a married couple), state death tax paid, foreign estate tax paid and prior estate tax paid on property received by the decedent within ten years before his or her death.

An estate tax return is required only if the estate plus lifetime gifts exceeds $5,250,000 (the amount which is tax free due to the applicable credit).

There is a provision of the income tax law that applies to property inherited from an estate. The deceased and the estate have paid no tax on any increase in value (appreciation or gain) since the property was acquired. The heir takes a "stepped-up" basis equal to fair value on the date of death. The result is nobody pays tax on the appreciation before the date of death.

GENERATION SKIPPING TRANSFER TAX

The generation skipping transfer tax ensures that estate tax is paid on property once each generation. This tax applies when property is given or willed to individuals one or more generations below the property owner (grandchildren, great grandchildren, etc.).

Each taxpayer has a $5,250,000 exemption for transfers before the tax is imposed (at a maximum rate of 40%). If property is transferred at death, estate tax as well as the generation skipping transfer tax is due. If the donor is alive when the property is given, the gift tax and the generation skipping transfer tax are due.

8 HIDDEN TAXES

Indirect taxes are included in the price of goods and services and thus are in a sense hidden from the individual who eventually pays the tax. Direct taxes include the estate and income taxes and payroll taxes such as the social security tax.

INFLATION

Inflation is a decline in the purchasing power of money over time. A dollar represents an obligation of the government owed to you which can be settled in real goods. If you hold a dollar during a period of inflation you will be able to purchase less in real goods at the end of that period than at the beginning.

Since the government owes you, and you receive less in real goods after inflation, the government settles the obligation with less real value than it owed at the beginning of the period. That decline in the real value of goods you receive is an economic gain to the government, a hidden tax.

Deflation is an increase in the purchasing power of money over time. However, if people and companies expect goods to cost more next year than this year they will defer purchases, decreasing current income and employment. Because of this economists warn governments to avoid deflation and instead attempt to create conditions for mild inflation of 1% or 2% per year. In that situation you know goods are likely to cost somewhat more next year than this year and you are motivated to buy now. Other people think the same way and those purchases lead to greater current employment.

Inflation is especially costly to savers. The larger your savings account the greater the decline in the real goods it will purchase during a period of inflation. Conversely, those who owe money, for example, a large mortgage on their home, will need less in real goods to acquire enough money to settle the mortgage after a period of inflation.

To reduce the risk of inflation people can invest in real estate and corporate stocks. They represent real goods and should theoretically maintain their value during inflation. Those who choose to invest in bonds (even government bonds) will be paid in money, and inflation will reduce the real value of those bonds over time. One response to this is the creation of inflation-protected bonds, which rise in monetary value over time to offset the risk of inflation. These bonds yield a lower interest rate than bonds that aren't inflation protected, but that may be a reasonable trade-off for people who expect significant inflation in the future.

STEALTH TAXES

In computing the individual income tax, total itemized deductions and exemptions are reduced for married taxpayers with AGI over $300,000. It represents a progressive increase in the income tax rates for higher income individuals. Similarly, the Medicare tax of 3.8% of investment income for higher income individuals (above $250,000 for married taxpayers) is buried in the tax form computations. These phase-outs of itemized deductions and exemptions and the Medicare tax on investment income for higher income taxpayers are not obvious from the tax form, so they are called stealth taxes.

GOVERNMENT OWNED BUSINESSES

Governments own corporations (such as casinos) which sometimes have significant profits. Those profits are hidden taxes since they accrue to the government, not to individuals. State sponsored gambling and lotteries are a hidden tax since, on average, the gamblers consistently lose and the states are the recipients of that wealth. Thomas Jefferson had this to say about lotteries: "...wherein the tax is laid on the willing only..."[26]

---

[26] Thomas Jefferson Randolph, *Memoir, correspondence, and miscellanies from the papers of Thomas Jefferson Volume III*, (Charlottesville, F. Carr and Co., 1829), 429.

And the willing turn out to be mainly those who can lease afford it. [27] States pay out only about half of lottery receipts in winnings[28], so on average the purchase of many lottery tickets is a money losing proposition. Studies show that the buyers of lottery tickets are relatively poor, and that many winners are not careful stewards of their newly acquired riches.

OTHER HIDDEN TAXES

Many excise taxes and import duties are indirect taxes and are hidden in a sense that they are not separately itemized to the purchaser of goods and services. This includes taxes on gasoline, diesel fuel, airplane tickets, car tires, alcohol, and tobacco. And, of course, import quotas represent a hidden tax because they indirectly result in an increase in the price due to a limit on the supply of goods and services.

HIDDEN SUBSIDIES IN TAXATION

It isn't just increases in taxes that are often hidden. Many provisions of the tax laws are subsidies for favored activities. Tax deductions for expenses not actually paid (such as percentage depletion expense above the cost of mineral property for investments like coal mines and oil and gas wells), tax favored treatment (lower tax rates) for long term capital gains and corporate dividends, tax-exempt interest income, deductions for some interest paid, and deductions for charitable contributions are all subsidies for these activities that are hidden in the tax law.

A more open way of supporting desired activities would be to take these provisions out of the tax law and have Congress vote to pay out government funds to those who engage in favored activities. Since the effect is the same (more money to those activities and less for the government) these hidden

---

[27] Emily Haisley, "Loving a bad bet: Factors that induce low-income individuals to purchase state lottery tickets",
<http://www.aeaweb.org/annual_mtg_papers/2008/2008_204.pdf>, (December 18, 2013)
[28] Ann E. Weiss, *Lotteries, Who Wins, Who Loses?*, (Hillside, N.J., Enslow, 1991), 65

subsidies are sometimes called "tax expenditures" even though no money was actually paid out for them.

If these tax expenditures were included in the budget as funds spent they could be compared with the costs of other programs and better decisions made about the costs of supporting various programs. One group of tax expenditures that is important to some taxpayers is the itemized deduction for mortgage interest and property tax, and the exclusion from gross income of gains from the sale of a principal residence.

And yet these tax breaks encourage people to own a home, which results in the risk of its value decreasing below the amount owed on the mortgage. Further, if a desirable job becomes available elsewhere it is much more difficult for the homeowner to move to take advantage of the new opportunity. These are significant risks to a homeowner and significant constraints on resource allocation to the economy as a whole

Those taxpayers who own residences are treated much differently than are other taxpayers in similar circumstances who rent an identical residence. If the government were to write a check to taxpayers each year for the value of these tax expenditures the unfairness of the difference would become quite apparent.

9 CHOOSING AN OPTIMAL TAX STRUCTURE

A nation's tax structure affects the economic choices people and companies make. But there is more to life than just dollars and economics. Perceived fairness is important, as is the cost of tax collection.

HOW TO CHOOSE

Two English philosophers, Jeremy Bentham and John Stuart Mill who lived in the 1800s, were utilitarians, arguing that the underlying moral criteria for decisions should be whether an alternative increases or decreases our happiness, and by how much. If an alternative increases economic productivity, but that increase in happiness is vastly outweighed by an increase in misery, that alternative ought not to be chosen. Can we agree that is the correct scale on which to base decisions about who to tax and how much to tax them? If not, what measure should we use to decide? [29]

It would seem that, if all else is equal, we would prefer to increase the overall happiness of all people impartially. In this case we are talking about people in the U.S., since our decisions are about the U.S. tax structure.

---

[29] For an extended discussion of this topic see Joshua Greene, (2013), *Moral Tribes: Emotion, Reason, and the Gap Between Us and Them*, Penguin Press

That leads to progressive taxation, since an extra dollar is less important to someone who makes $200,000 a year than it is to someone making $20,000. So as income and wealth increase, tax rates should increase. Property taxes and sales taxes (regressive) are less desirable than income and estate taxes with increasing rates (progressive) using the criteria of maximizing overall happiness. When property taxes are used there should be provisions to reduce taxes for those with lower incomes. And sales taxes should not apply to the purchase of basic groceries and medicines.

Making the tax system more progressive by raising rates at the top income levels and also decreasing rates near the bottom will increase economic activity and employment. How? People at the bottom spend almost every additional dollar they have available, while people at the top don't find much more they want to buy and save a significant portion. Thus, making the tax structure more progressive adds jobs to the economy without increasing total tax receipts.

DOES INCREASING TAXES DECREASE NATIONAL INCOME?

Northern European countries provide excellent infrastructure, universal education through college or university, and universal health care, which makes their tax burden much greater than in the U.S. People sometimes argue that these higher taxes will stifle work and innovation.

But consider Sweden, one of those high taxing countries. In 2012 Sweden took 44.3% of GDP in taxes, while the U.S. took only 24.3% that year. [30] GDP per capita in Sweden in constant dollars increased by 98% from 2000 to 2012, while per capita GDP in the low tax U.S. only increased 42%, during that period of *declining* U.S. income and estate tax rates. [31] [32]

---

[30] Organization for Economic Co-operation and Development Revenue Statistics – Comparative Tables from http://stats.oecd.org/Index.aspx?DataSetCode=REV (December 30, 2013)

[31] World Bank Indicators (GDP per capita by year and country in 2013 U.S. dollars adjusted for inflation) from http://data.worldbank.org/indicator/NY.GDP.MKTP.CD (December 13, 2013)

[32] Edmund L. Andrews, "Tax Cuts Offer Most for Very Rich, Study Says", *New York Times,* January 8, 2007

Northern Europeans argue that those expenditures for health, education, and infrastructure make their populations much more productive.

During the presidency of Bill Clinton taxes were increased and the economy boomed, resulting in the budget deficit becoming a budget surplus by the end of his time in office. On the other hand, the presidency of George W. Bush started with huge tax cuts and ended by changing that budget surplus he started with back to a huge deficit. There are other factors to consider, such as the end of the cold war at the beginning of Clinton's presidency, and the Iraq and Afghanistan wars under Bush, but the overall pattern clearly refutes claims of the right that a tax cut pays for itself. [33]

DOES AUSTERITY WORK?

Those on the right argue that decreasing government spending will increase confidence and lead to more investment and more jobs. History shows it just doesn't work. Austerity led to the great depression and it is currently keeping us in a recession much longer than necessary. In a period of high unemployment government spending puts people to work and they happily spend that income, which puts more people to work. That leads to more tax revenue which covers some of the cost of the government spending. [34]

EDUCATION

U.S. high school students perform miserably in comparison to many other countries, especially in science and math, skills more and more important in todays competitive world where jobs are easily moved from one country to another. This starts at pre-kindergarten and elementary schools, where the U.S. invests little compared to countries more successful at educating their future workers. Those future workers will be the ones generating income to support themselves as well as the increasing number who are retiring (our social security system is a "pay-as-you-go" system, with very little set aside for future benefits).

---

[33] Albert R. Hunt, "Do Lower Taxes Create Jobs? Look At Clinton And Bush", *New York Times*, December 16, 2012

[34] Joseph E. Stiglitz, *The Price of Inequality: How Today's Divided Society Endangers Our Future*, (Norton 2012), 230

Sweden averages 19.2 years of formal education, Australia averages 18.5 years, while the U.S. averages only 17.1 years. [35] Denmark spends 2.3% of GDP on its labor market policies, including extensive retraining for its unemployed. The U.S. spends only 0.1%, about what is spent by Chile. [36]

An obvious investment that will improve the wellbeing and happiness of the U.S. population as a whole would be to invest far more in preschool, elementary, and secondary education, especially in less wealthy school districts. Investing in preschool not only improves the productivity of the future workforce, it frees up parents of those children to join the formal workforce. Community colleges joining with businesses in apprenticeship programs have been proven in other countries (especially Germany) to increase the supply of trained workers for jobs that don't require a four year degree but which lead to comfortable middle income jobs. To support these goals a tax on wealthier people and those with the highest incomes would reduce their happiness today much less than it would increase the happiness of the country as a whole in the future.

This increased investment must be used wisely. Studies consistently show that students of the best teachers do far better than those of mediocre teachers. How do we take advantage of this fact? By restructuring our colleges of education to admit only the best students and increasing the pay of the best teachers so the top students want to join their ranks. Our country over-invests in financial wizards (OK, we will still need a few experts in taxation) but clearly underinvests in its teachers.

One important change to our public education system is to revise its funding. We now spend much more in wealthy school districts than in poorer ones. Statewide funding, to equalize spending per student between wealthy schools and those in poorer areas, would make a big difference in giving talented students from all sectors the opportunity to benefit from the best education we can offer them.

Other countries (Finland, recruit the best teachers and challenge them in university, and the results show up in international test rankings when students are compared. People in those countries don't understand our

---

[35] Organization for Economic Co-operation and Development (OECD), OECD Better Life Index, http://www.oecdbetterlifeindex.org/topics/education/ (December 16, 2013)
[36] "Unemployment – Long time gone", *The Economist*, Jan. 4, 2014, 19.

sports culture. Kids there play soccer, but informally in clubs, not on varsity teams. We have our priorities wrong to successfully compete in todays integrated world.[37]

CORPORATE TAX INCENTIVES

A corporation is not taxed on the income from foreign subsidiaries until it is remitted to the U.S. This allows many large corporations to permanently avoid U.S. income tax by moving their most profitable operations to their subsidiaries in other countries that have low income tax rates, encouraging them to invest in other countries instead of in the U.S.

Why do we not extend the corporate income tax to the income of all components of companies that operate in the U.S., no matter where in the world they are located and when they choose to remit dividends to the U.S.?

CARBON EMISSIONS

The United States is on the cusp of significant changes in climate and natural resources due to global warming. Higher temperatures, more droughts, increased storminess, expanded insect attacks on forests, more severe wildfires, and drought effects on agriculture may be early warning signs of changes that will accompany a permanently warmer world. These changes will affect people and economies in many ways.

It isn't just left-leaning academics who are thinking seriously about the costs of global warming due to human carbon emissions. Many companies are already considering this cost in their internal planning, pricing carbon emissions at amounts ranging from $6 a ton to $60 a ton, depending on the life expected from the project (they are assuming their cost of carbon emissions will rise as time passes). These aren't just green companies. Exxon Mobile and Shell, very large oil companies, and Delta Airlines are doing this too. [38]

---

[37] Amanda Ripley, *The Smartest Kids in the World: And How They Got That Way*, (New York, Simon & Schuster, 2013)

[38] "Carbon Copy - Companies and emissions", *The Economist*, December 14, 2013

Companies are also noticing periodic supply chain shortages indirectly caused by global warming and resulting unstable costs. Nike and Coke are worried enough about this to take action. [39]

An excise tax on carbon (call it a sin tax if you like), is one way to mitigate our addiction to fossil fuels, making it more expensive to purchase goods and services that result in carbon emissions. For example, air travel emits more carbon than almost any other human activity, followed by driving vehicles and heating buildings. Using cement and steel in construction requires 10 times more carbon than using wood.

Placing an economic value on carbon would provide an incentive to modify behaviors that exacerbate carbon emissions, reduce the rate of global warming, and buy some time to develop alternative energy sources and technology (solar, wind, bioenergy, etc.). This tax could also be used to reduce other taxes or invested in deteriorating infrastructure, education, and other enterprises that benefit the economy and enrich our quality of life.[40]

This carbon tax could be instituted at a low level, but scheduled to automatically increase each year in the future. This would give people time to plan for changes in the economy. [41] It would lead to loss of jobs in coal mining regions, but that would be more than offset by increases in jobs in regions with wind, solar, and nuclear power and energy from biomass.

Coal miners could be encouraged to retrain for jobs as electricians or construction workers. Large investments in power lines to carry the power from producing regions to cities will be needed. Investors will need to reallocate their investment portfolios.[42] Companies will choose to invest in those growing sectors of the economy. Individuals and companies will invest in electric cars and hybrids as well as rooftop solar panels. Government

---

[39] Coral Davenport, "Industry Awakens to Threat of Climate Change", *New York Times*, Jan. 23, 2014
[40] David L. Peterson, U.S. Forest Service forestry research scientist and member of the Intergovernmental Panel on Climate Change (IPCC), e-mail to author, December 14, 2013
[41] See the Wikipedia article "Carbon Tax"
[42] Carbon Tax Center, *Pricing carbon efficiently and equitably*, http://www.carbontax.org (December 15, 2013)

incentives are unlikely to be needed if the carbon tax makes the economics of low carbon versus high carbon energy sources clear. [43]

The U.S. is fortunate to have a rising supply of inexpensive natural gas. Trucking companies are already converting fleets of diesel powered trucks to run on natural gas, saving more on fuel than the cost of the conversion.[44] Since natural gas produces about half the carbon emissions of coal for the same energy production, natural gas is an obvious bridge technology to a low carbon economy for electricity production as well as transportation.[45]

Finally, the percentage depletion allowed to the owners of coal, oil, and natural gas properties (the fictitious deduction of an expense that was never paid out), lowering their income tax, should be eliminated, as should other tax incentives for such properties.

INFRASTRUCTURE AND BASIC RESEARCH

The American Society of Civil Engineers issued a comprehensive report card on the maintenance of our roads, bridges, railways, ports, and other infrastructure. They gave the U.S. a maintenance grade of D+. This is a disgrace in such a wealthy country with so many out of work due to the great recession. [46]

Borrowing to upgrade our infrastructure is a logical investment which will put people to work now, helping our struggling economy and generating a return due to reduced maintenance and improved efficiency in the future. Those savings will be available to pay back the debt invested in the infrastructure and will increase future tax receipts as well. The engineers estimate an

---

[43] Center for Climate and Electricity Policy, Considering a Carbon Tax: Frequently Asked Questions, http://www.rff.org/centers/climate_and_electricity_policy/pages/carbon_tax_faqs.aspx (December 15, 2013)
[44] Diane Cardwell and Clifford Krauss, "Trucking Industry Is Set to Expand Its Use of Natural Gas", *New York Times*, April 22, 2013
[45] Beth Gardiner, "Is Natural Gas Good, or Just Less Bad"?, *New York Times*, February 22, 2011
[46] John Schwartz, "Small Infrastructure Gains Are Observed in Engineering Report", *New York Times*, March 19, 2013

investment of $3.6 trillion is needed by 2020 to bring our infrastructure up to sustainable condition.

It makes sense to borrow to invest in infrastructure now when interest rates are at historically low levels and the economy has slack capacity. Putting these repairs off until later will likely mean spending much more then. There is little doubt that overall happiness will be increased by borrowing to invest in these needed repairs now.

Other countries (China, Japan, Europe) have invested significantly in high speed rail. A similar investment in the U.S. could save a tremendous amount of carbon emissions by substituting high speed rail for plane travel, in many cases reducing the time needed for door-to-door travel. This seems an obvious investment to reduce carbon emissions.

The U.S. compares badly with other countries in the installation of broad band Internet. Such investment would improve the productivity of our companies and enable more use of technology in far flung schools. The long term return on such an investment in our relative competitiveness with other countries is likely to be quite high, an investment we really can't afford not to make. [47]

GOVERNMENT SUPPORTED RESEARCH

Basic research supported by government in the U.S. has led to an unbelievably diverse range of improvements to our lives, from the Internet, to life-saving drugs, to the safety of our highways. In recent years this investment has been declining and the result will be fewer discoveries that companies can use to further improve our lives. Increasing taxes on the wealthy and investing the money in more research will give society as a whole a much greater rate of return than if it were left in private hands. Continuing to decrease spending on basic research is a self-defeating way of saving money.

One study showed a rate of return on government supported basic research of about 50%, greatly above the 20-30% rate of return on privately funded

---

[47] Edward Wyatt, "U.S. Struggles To Keep Pace in Delivering Broadband Service", *New York Times*, December 29, 2013

research. [48] The government can currently borrow at interest rates close to zero. Spending on research is a logical thing to do, whether financed by taxation or borrowing.

TAX FAVORITES

Some income is taxed at a lower effective rate than other income. For example, the rules allow recipients of income from minerals, like coal, oil and gas, to deduct percentage depletion, often allowing deductions over several years in excess of the actual cost of the property.

Long term capital gains and dividends from C-type corporations are taxed at a maximum of 15% (20% for individuals in the top tax bracket of 39.6%). Even more surprising to most taxpayers, when property is inherited from an estate the heir takes a "stepped-up" basis equal to fair value on the date of death. The result is nobody pays tax on the appreciation before the date of death and any appreciation after that date is generally taxed as a long-term capital gain at a maximum of 20%.

This results in two similar taxpayers paying very different amounts of tax. One who sells an asset while alive pays tax on the gain, while one who leaves the same asset to heirs avoids paying tax on the gain entirely. Doing away with the stepped up basis and taxing C-type dividends and long-term capital gains at the ordinary income rate (up to 39.6%) would improve the perceived horizontal equity of the income tax law.

NONPROFIT ORGANIZATIONS

According to the Urban Institute's National Center for Charitable Statistics, nonprofit organizations contributed 5.4 percent of the country's Gross Domestic Product in 2009, and they held a total of $4.3 trillion in assets, up from $2.4 trillion in 1999 -- a 39% increase after adjusting for inflation over just ten years. [49] Many of the investments of nonprofits and charitable foundations are in corporate stock.

---

[48] The Council of Economic Advisers, "Supporting Research and Development to Promote Economic Growth: The Federal Government's Role", October 1995

[49] Waqas Naeem, "Nonprofit organizations have become an important part of

Economists criticize the corporate income tax as being double taxation, since the corporation pays the corporate income tax and dividends from the corporation are also taxed to individual stockholders. However, nonprofits benefit from government services as do individuals. Since they pay no income tax themselves one way for nonprofits to share in the cost of supporting government is for the corporation to pay the corporate income tax before distributing dividends to nonprofits.

Nonprofit organizations such as churches, schools, and hospitals often don't pay property taxes. Over time the percentage of such property in some cities has increased significantly as manufacturers and retailers have moved to the suburbs, which reduces the percentage of property in the city that is subject to property tax. For example, over half the property in Boston is owned by nonprofits.[50] Some cities are starting to charge fees (in lieu of taxes) to nonprofits for services such as water, fire, streets, and police. The choice is to either impose such fees on nonprofits or raise taxes on taxable property to unsustainable levels.

Charities, like corporations, benefit from government services such as a stable legal system that enforces contracts, roads, fire and police departments, and schools that educate workers that will be employed by the charity in the future. An effective way to assure that the full costs of those services are borne by donors and that the ultimate consumers of the services pay the cost of those government services is to tax the charity for the value of those services.

CHARITABLE CONTRIBUTIONS

If the income of charities were taxed it would increase equity of taxation and the efficiency in resource allocation. By broadening the tax base income tax rates could be significantly reduced for society as a whole. It would also charge charities for externalities that are caused by operations of the charity. Many activities cause costs to be born by others, such as global warming due

---

the U.S. economy", *TimesRecordNews,* Wichita Falls, Texas, May 20, 2012

[50] Michael Cooper, "Squeezed Cities Ask Nonprofits for More Money", *New York Times,* May 11, 2011

to carbon emissions. Taxing a charity that uses an inefficient furnace to heat its office at the source of the emissions might be the most efficient and effective way of assuring that the donors and consumers of the charity's services will tend to reduce harmful externalities as well as encourage the supporters of the organization to consider replacing the polluting furnace with a more environmentally friendly alternative.

In recent years charity ranking organizations have been ranking charities on efficiency; the percentage of their contributions that are used for program purposes and the percentage used for fundraising and administration. But little is known about the effectiveness of their expenditures, meaning donors have little information to use in choosing which charities to support. Some charities are clearly misleading donors since they pay 70% to 90% of their donations to for-profit fundraisers to raise more funds.[51] Why do we allow tax deductions for contributions to such inefficient charities?

The estate tax and income tax deductions for charitable contributions primarily benefit those in the top tax brackets – most of those with lower incomes use the standard deduction and don't itemize, so don't specifically deduct their charitable contributions. And the higher the tax bracket the greater the amount of tax saved per dollar of contribution. Someone in the 15% tax bracket saves 15 cents per dollar contributed, while someone in the 39.6% bracket saves 39.6 cents for each dollar. Why should society contribute $396 toward a $1,000 charitable contribution for a wealthy donor compared to $150 toward the same contribution for a donor of more modest means? And society contributes nothing toward the same $1,000 contribution made by a taxpayer who takes the standard deduction instead of itemizing. This structure makes no logical sense at all.

Higher income individuals have an incentive to overstate the value of appreciated long term capital assets donated to charities. If they sold the asset they would be taxed on the increase in value. But if they donate the asset directly to a charity they can deduct the full fair market value, saving $39.60 per $100 of value contributed for taxpayers in the 39.6% income tax bracket. Lower income taxpayers are not only less likely to own appreciated assets, they would save less in tax from the donation due to their lower incremental tax bracket.

---

[51] Charity Navigator, *10 Charities Overpaying their For-Profit Fundraisers*, http://www.charitynavigator.org/index.cfm?bay=topten.detail&listid=28#.UrBMBqW5duY (December 17, 2013)

Not all countries allow deductions for charitable contributions. Austria, Finland and Sweden do not allow income tax deductions for charitable contributions. Denmark, Finland, Norway and Sweden do not allow estate tax deductions for charitable contributions.[52]

In the U.S., not only are charitable contributions deductible on an income tax return, but charitable donations specified in a will are deductible in computing the estate tax.

Why should choosing to make charitable contributions be treated differently than choosing to spend money on other things? Are charitable contributions preferable to public expenditures for scientific research, infrastructure and education? It seems unlikely that they benefit society more in total, leading to the conclusion that deductions for charitable contributions in both the income tax and the estate tax would be eliminated in a more rational tax structure.

INEQUALITY

Income growth in the U.S. in recent years has benefitted those already at the top of the income pyramid almost entirely. Income for the lower earners has stagnated, leading to a few people with far more resources than they can spend and many people with very little. The top 10% in America now take home 50% of our national income, drastically more than the third they earned in 1979. Even more surprising, in 2012 the top 1% in income took home over 23% of our national income, the same as just before the stock market crash of 1929. Their share went down below 10% in the 1970s, but has risen steadily since.[53]

Productivity of American workers has increased significantly in recent years, but those productivity gains have not been passed on to workers. Productivity rose by 22 percent from 2000 to 2012, while wages increased by only 7.7

---

[52] David Roodman and Scott Standley, Center for Global Development, Working Paper Number 82, "Tax policies to promote private charitable giving in DAC countries", (January 2006), page 15

[53] Emmanuel Saez, *Striking it Richer: The Evolution of Top Incomes in the United States*, http://elsa.berkeley.edu/~saez/saez-UStopincomes-2012.pdf (December 15, 2013)

percent. [54] Competition by workers in other countries who are paid less than U.S. workers explain much of this anomaly.

Recent research analyzing rates of return on capital and concentrations of wealth over hundreds of years result in the predicted inequality increasing significantly as the population ages and population growth slows over the coming years.[55] Tax policy can help reduce this expected increase in inequality.

Conservatives claimed that lower tax rates result in more investment and more jobs. The evidence is overwhelming that this is untrue. [56] Would increasing taxes on those at the top lower their happiness a larger amount than the increase in happiness that could result from a reduction in taxes of those at the bottom?

Mitt Romney had a famously low 13.9% average tax rate on his 2010 income of over $13,000,000. How did he accomplish this, paying a lower tax rate than many who make much less, when tax rates on ordinary income went as high as 35%? Investors like him have a provision in the tax law called "carried interest" that allows them to convert ordinary income to long term capital gains and corporate dividends, both of which are now taxed at a maximum of 20%, while avoiding the social security tax imposed on ordinary income. [57] Normal people aren't likely to perceive the tax law as being fair as long as it contains exceptions like this 20% carried interest tax rate.

Warren Buffet is one of the wealthiest people in the world, yet claims to pay a much lower tax rate than his secretary. In 2010 he says his tax rate was half that of the 20 other people in his office, who all make much less than he does. [58]

---

[54] Steven Rattner, "America in 2013, as Told in Charts," *New York Times*, December 30, 2013

[55] "Free Exchange - All men are created unequal", *The Economist,* January 4, 2014, 60

[56] Joseph E. Stiglitz, *The Price of Inequality: How Today's Divided Society Endangers Our Future*, (Norton 2012), 71

[57] Nicholas Confessore and David Kocieniewski, "For Romneys, Friendly Code Reduces Taxes", *New York Times,* January 24, 2012

[58] Warren E. Buffett, "Stop Coddling the Super-Rich", *New York Times,* August 14, 2011

France has raised their top income tax rate (on salaries above 1,000,000 Euros or $1,373,000) to 75% and their top court has upheld the tax. [59] The highest income tax rate in the U.S. was over 90% from 1944 until 1964. During that period the U.S. started building the Interstate Highway system. Today that highway system cries out for repairs and our maximum income tax rate is 39.6%.

Taxing long term capital gains and corporate dividends at the same rate as ordinary income would reduce the almost unbelievably preferential treatment of the most wealthy taxpayers.[60] This increase in tax receipts could more than pay for eliminating payroll taxes on people earning close to minimum wage, which would increase the happiness of those at the bottom far more than it would decrease the happiness of Mr. Romney and Mr. Buffett.

The maximum estate tax rate was 77% from 1941 to 1969. Today it is 40%. This allows the descendants of wealthy individuals to live a life of ease with no need to work, depriving the economy of the contributions that these often talented and well educated individuals could make. What inventions could they have come up with that we are doing without? Significantly increasing the rate on the largest fortunes would raise revenue that could be invested in education and infrastructure. This would increase the future happiness of society as a whole. How much would such an increase decrease the happiness of those who would inherit tens of millions instead of hundreds of millions of dollars?

Stockholders often benefit from share buyback plans when their corporation repurchases its own shares instead of paying a cash dividend. Shareholders can continue to hold shares that have increased in value (paying no income tax currently), donate them for an income tax deduction, or leave them to heirs in their estate. These last two alternatives allow the income tax to be avoided permanently. The gain isn't taxed when appreciated shares are donated to a charity, and the fair value can be claimed as an itemized deduction. Heirs receive a "stepped-up" basis, meaning the deceased never paid income tax on the gain, the estate never paid income tax on the gain, and the heir never pays income tax on the gain. That "stepped-up" basis rule

---

[59] "France's 75% tax rate gains approval by top court", *BBC News*, 29 December 2013
[60] Joseph E. Stiglitz, *The Price of Inequality: How Today's Divided Society Endangers Our Future*, (Norton 2012), 71

should be changed so either the deceased or the heir pays income tax on the increase in value of the stock.

As these giant fortunes are passed to later generations they keep growing, making the inequalities in our society more and more obvious to everyone. The alternative of investing revenue from an increase in estate taxes in quality education will provide greater productivity from that smarter work force than leaving the wealth in the hands of a few.

It is possible to make employees into owners which would decrease inequality over time. At one time our tax code included tax benefits for Employee Stock Ownership Plans (ESOPs) but those have mostly been eliminated. Studies have shown that companies with such plans are more productive than other companies because employees are motivated to consider the effects of decisions on the value of their own stock. We might want to make such plans a part of our investment in the future of the country.[61]

Property tax rates vary greatly across states and across the country. Horizontal equity could be considerably improved by subjecting all property in a state (or even across the country) to consistent valuations, rules and rates. School districts funded by the same statewide property taxes could give students in less prosperous communities opportunities similar to those from wealthier communities, leading to a more efficient economy that gives all students the chance to rise to their potential.

POLITICAL INFLUENCE OF THE WEALTHY

How has our tax system gotten into the deplorable condition described above? Wealthy people can afford to make large political contributions and hire the most talented lobbying and public relations firms. The poor and middle class can't afford the campaign contributions and lobbyists that are so well supported by the very wealthy.

Members of the very wealthy (the 1%) feel they've earned what they have and it shouldn't be taken away from them. But they've gotten it by relying on our publicly supported research and infrastructure and they've kept it because the

---

[61] Thomas B. Edsall, "Whatever Happened to 'Every Man a King'?", *New York Times*, Feb. 11, 2014

legal structure of our society protects their property rights. There are other countries where they wouldn't feel so comfortable displaying their extreme wealth. It doesn't seem unfair to ask those who benefit the most from the protections we enjoy to contribute significantly in return.

When a member of Congress receives regular large campaign contributions there may be no obvious corruption. But everyone involved knows of the expectation, that the member will vote for legislation favored by those donors, and if those votes aren't forthcoming then the campaign contributions will dry up.

The wealthy have captured parts of our news media and, with the aid of their excellent public relations people, have slanted the messages of that news media toward politicians and programs favored by the wealthy and by large corporations. One approach to shining some light on this situation is to do away with the political entities that aren't required to disclose who their donors are and the amount of the donations. [62] If we did that at least we wouldn't be left in the dark as to who the big donors are.

The focused message of right wing news outlets has resulted in strange outcomes. Many of those on the right who are staunchly opposed to the estate tax haven't studied it deeply enough to understand that there is almost no chance it will apply to their own estate. An individual must have assets over $5,250,000 ($10,500,000 for a married couple) for their estate to be subject to the tax. Why would they oppose a tax that will never impact them or their family?

The right argues that the estate tax will force the sale of family owned small businesses or farms. But most family owned small businesses and farms aren't large enough to subject the estate to the tax. And if the tax does apply the estate can elect to defer the tax for five years and then pay it in 10 annual installments. The tax is structured to do what it is intended to do, to tax the estates of the very wealthy, but the right has focused its message on the dreaded "death tax" to persuade many to oppose the tax, even though their family will never be subject to it.

---

[62] Mike Mcintire And Nicholas Confessore, "Tax-Exempt Groups Shield Political Gifts of Businesses", *New York Times*, July 7, 2012

In some states the wealthy have made voting more difficult by requiring specific identification documents that are difficult for the poor to obtain. They've also limited voting hours, and limited the number of voting booths. This has biased the selection of people who actually vote and increased the likelihood of electing those favored by the more wealthy in our society.

There are ways to overcome this problem. Several states have found one that actually saves money. Elections are conducted by mail, and booklets with balanced commentary (including the effects on the state budget of proposed laws) are mailed to voters before the election so voters have time to read and discuss the alternatives.[63] Washington and Oregon have moved all elections to mail ballots and found it less expensive than traditional voting. They've also found that they are able to address voter fraud better than at traditional balloting locations. Even better they've had higher voter participation, often near the highest in the nation. [64]

Contributions by the wealthy have supported gerrymandering of voting districts to make election of a member of a favored political party almost certain. [65] If voting district maps were drawn by independent bodies so they don't favor one party or the other we'd have legislatures more representative of the actual will of the voters.

The 1% are able to disguise their ownership of trusts and corporations through shell entities and the use of tax havens. If laws required disclosure of the beneficial owners of such entities (those who ultimately receive the money and other benefits), tax equity and enforcement would be improved. That could result in lower taxes for the rest of the population.

The wealthy can disguise their political contributions through nonprofit entities. If major donors to political organizations were disclosed the public could know which of the wealthy are supporting which proposals and evaluate them with that in mind.

---

[63] "Voting by Mail", *New York Times*, October 6, 2012
[64] "LETTERS Sunday Dialogue: To Enhance Democracy, Expand Vote-by-Mail, Letter to the editor from Phil Keisling, former Oregon secretary of state and chief elections official", *New York Times*, October 20, 2012
[65] Sam Wang, "The Great Gerrymander of 2012", *New York Times*, February 2, 2013

Albert K. Francisco

10 CONCLUSION

Government services are necessary, not optional. We wouldn't like living in a society with no firefighters, no police, no military, and no public schools. Government services cost money and somebody has to bear that cost. Either we pay for those services now or we borrow and pay back the debt later. Most people think it fair that our tax system is progressive, that those with more income pay a higher percentage of their income as taxes than those with less income. Our system of taxation is just one of many in the world and it makes sense to consider what is working in other places.

COUNTRIES LEARNING FROM EACH OTHER

A vast majority of other countries have adopted a Value Added Tax (VAT). We might ask why it is so widely adopted and whether it would be appropriate to replace some of our current tax structure with a VAT. Economists argue that the efficiency of collection, and the desirability of taxing consumption (instead of work and savings) make the VAT score high when compared to other tax systems.

Some countries have been eliminating the exemption from taxation of employee fringe benefits. Employers tend to move compensation from cash wages to fringe benefits when those benefits aren't taxed. Economists point out that specific fringe benefits aren't valuable to some employees (subsidized daycare is useless to employees who have no dependents, while parking and public transit subsidies don't help those who walk or bike to work). Such benefits are an inefficient way to compensate employees when some don't benefit from them.

The U.S. differs from other countries in that we use deductions, exclusions, and credits to reduce taxes for many items that would be specific government expenditures elsewhere. [66] These "tax expenditures" may not be the most effective or efficient way to encourage those activities. Paying a direct cash subsidy to support desired activities makes the support more visible than a hidden subsidy in the tax rules, giving legislators and citizens a better chance to weigh in on the desirability of the subsidy.

In some countries, such as Great Britain, the vast majority of taxpayers have no need to file an income tax return since the withholding at the source of their income is equal to the tax owed. Only taxpayers with income from other sources need bother filling out the forms. [67] The U.S. might consider moving toward such a system to reduce the costs of compliance and administration of the tax law and the negative attitude toward taxes that invariably results after the effort of filling out the complex forms currently required by the individual income tax.

We can't demand that other countries institute the same tax structure that we use in the U.S. However, distant parts of the world are today finding themselves closer together in uncomfortable ways. It doesn't matter if carbon is emitted in the U.S. or elsewhere, it still has the same effect on global warming, so should be discouraged to reduce future damage from climate change.

If we institute a significant carbon tax here we can also impose it as an import duty at our borders. Goods produced outside the U.S. can be taxed based on their estimated carbon emissions just as if they were produced here. That would, of course, include the carbon emissions from ships or planes used to bring them to our borders. This might lead to increased employment in the U.S. since those transportation carbon emissions would increase the cost of imported goods as compared to domestically produced goods.

---

[66] Victor Thuronyi, *Comparative Tax Law*, (Kluwer Law International, The Hague, The Netherlands, 2003), 15

[67] Cedric Sandford, *Why Tax Systems Differ*, (Fiscal Publications, Bath, England, 2000), 148

Countries that institute similar carbon taxes could be given credits against the U.S. tax so the goods aren't taxed both there and here. This would put imports and domestic production on the same basis and strongly encourage other countries to institute a carbon tax, leading to more reductions in global carbon emissions.

SPECIFIC TAX PROGRAMS IN OTHER COUNTRIES

> "When it comes to healthy eating as measured by diabetes and obesity rates, we're 120th: sixth from the bottom, better off only than Saudi Arabia, Kuwait, Jordan, Fiji and our unlucky neighbor Mexico." [68]

If the recently imposed tax on sugary drinks and junk food in Mexico has the intended effect of decreasing calorie consumption and obesity, leading to better health in the population, we might consider a similar tax here. [69]

Switzerland is voting (as of 2014) on whether to institute a minimum income for all citizens, to eliminate poverty.[70] The U.S. might consider this too, replacing food stamps, welfare, unemployment benefits, supplemental housing benefits, school lunch, and similar programs (and the bureaucracies that administer them), perhaps saving money when compared to today's complex benefits structure.

This proposal is supported by some on the left as well as some on the right. Conservatives like the idea of eliminating the large bureaucracy that administers our social welfare programs. They also like the idea of untying our current social welfare programs from specific states and cities to allow the poor to move from areas with high unemployment to places with plenty of jobs. They argue that our society would be better served by encouraging citizens to move to take jobs that might otherwise go to immigrants.[71]

---

[68] Mark Bittman, "Abundance Doesn't Mean Health", *New York Times,* Jan. 21, 2014

[69] Paulina Villega, "Mexico: Junk Food Tax Is Approved," *New York Times,* October 31, 2013

[70] Annie Lowrey, "Switzerland's Proposal to Pay People for Being Alive", *New York Times*, November 12, 2013

[71] Eli Lehrer And Lori Sanders, "Moving to Work", *National Affairs,* Number 18, Winter 2014

Liberals like the idea of eliminating poverty, so with support from both the left and the right this has a chance of happening.

A guaranteed income might result in a disincentive for working, but if the minimum income were just enough to live on, but not enough to live especially comfortably, that disincentive may be minimal. And it would give those in school and those trying to start a business a chance to achieve their dreams, possibly leading to a much more productive economy. We already have the successful earned income credit `(negative income tax) that writes a check to low income earners each year through the income tax law, so the administrative system is already in place.

Should the guaranteed income be increased for families with children? Several recent scientific studies have shown that increased family financial support in early childhood significantly improves parental nurturing by decreasing stresses on the parents. It also results in improved social outcomes for the children as they grow up and that evidence is supported by MRI brain studies. Finally, the evidence suggests the costs of early support are more than returned by later savings to society from reduced crime and increased abilities of children as they become adults. [72]

Our wealthy country should be proud to be able to eliminate panhandlers with "help – I'm homeless" signs.

SUBSIDIZED CHILD CARE

In Sweden, public preschools allow parents to continue work or studies and foster children's learning. Preschool starts at age 1, even when parents aren't working, at no charge for a basic number of hours. Generally preschools are open from 6:30 a.m. until 6:30 p.m., with some open holidays, nights, and weekends to serve parents who work then.

Fees are based on family income, with a maximum of $196 per month. The result is that 94% of Swedish children between 3 and 5 are enrolled. Sweden

---

[72] Moises Velasquez-Manoff, "The Great Divide: What Happens When The Poor Receive A Stipend?", *New York Times,* January 18, 2014

has close to the highest employment rates of women and mothers and the lowest child poverty level in the world.

If a similar program were adopted in the U.S. we'd reduce poverty by giving low income parents the opportunity to start businesses, work, or go to school. We'd improve the abilities of the kids in preschool to contribute to the economy when they grow up.[73] In Sweden the program is tax financed. Could we do the same in the U.S., giving unemployed people useful jobs in child care and investing in the capabilities of our current and future workforce? This seems to be an investment where the payback undoubtedly exceeds the cost.

EDUCATING CITIZENS OF OTHER COUNTRIES

The U.S. has had a system of colleges and universities that is the envy of the world. Many very intelligent citizens of other countries come to the U.S. for higher education. This is one of the best investments we can make in the future happiness of the world as a whole. When they return home they better understand democracy and help spread our freedoms worldwide. Some are able to stay in the U.S. and start successful businesses, leading to jobs and innovations that improve our economy. Today state governments are in budgetary strait-jackets and many have been forced to greatly reduce funding for their excellent colleges and universities.

Both U.S. citizens and those of other countries here for higher education are finding our schools noticeably declining in quality and increasing in cost. Supplementing our investments in higher education with funds from a carbon tax and more progressive income and estate taxes will improve future incomes and happiness in both the U.S. and other countries. The proliferation of classes available on the Internet at minimal or no cost is a way of making our knowledge more widely available at reasonable cost, but someone must produce those high quality courses and that takes significant investment in universities.

---

[73] Miriam Nordfors, "Room for Debate: Sweden Solves Two Problems at Once", *New York Times*, February 28, 2013

Albert K. Francisco

POTENTIAL CHANGES TO CONSIDER IN OUR TAX SYSTEM

Our tax system in the U.S. has been created over centuries and is a very inefficient way to raise the revenue needed to fund public services. There are many changes that could reduce the cost of collecting revenue for public services and at the same time nudge the population to make changes in their lifestyles that could decrease misery and increase the happiness of our citizens.

Some of these changes are alternatives to each other while others are stand-alone modifications to the system. These possible changes include:

VAT, EXCISE and SALES TAX		
ACTION	RESULT	PAGE
High tax on alcohol content of drinks	Improved health Longer lives	9
Increase federal tobacco taxes	Improved health Longer lives	9
Tax sugary soft drinks and junk food	Improved health Longer lives	9, 63
Value Added Tax nationwide to replace state/local sales tax	Increase collection efficiency, decrease regional inequity	17
Carbon tax within VAT for common reporting	Reduce long term global warming impact	47
Institute tax on agricultural fertilizer	Reduce river runoff and ocean dead zones, improving fishing and safety of seafood produced	11

INDIVIDUAL INCOME TAX		
ACTION	RESULT	PAGE
Higher incremental income tax rate on top 1%	Reduce inequality	54
Eliminate low capital gains tax rate	Reduce inequality by increasing vertical equity	51
Tax corporate dividend income at ordinary income tax rate	Reduce inequality by increasing vertical equity	51
Eliminate income tax exclusion for employee fringe benefits	Reduce incentive to pay employees with benefits that are less valuable to them than	61

	cash wages	
Stock option income taxed at ordinary tax rates	Reduced emphasis on short term results by corporate executives	31
Change "tax expenditures" to government cash expenditures requiring legislative approval	Improve disclosure of the costs to society and open public debate	41
Tax asset appreciation as ordinary income at death	Eliminate opportunity for tax avoidance in current "stepped up basis"	37
Eliminate percentage depletion deduction for mineral property	Limit deduction to actual cost paid, improving tax equity	30
Change the income tax exemption from a deduction to a credit	Makes the tax less regressive (increases vertical equity)	26
Structure income tax so most taxpayers need file no return	Reduce cost of compliance and enforcement; reduce negative attitude toward taxes from completing tax return	62
Make tax exempt interest income, capital gains, and corporate dividends minimum tax preferences	Increase horizontal equity by treating people with similar income in the same way	34
Tax stock options as ordinary income when granted	Eliminate opportunity for deferral or avoidance of significant income tax	31
Guaranteed income for all citizens as a negative income tax	Improve health, reduce inequality, and bureaucracy, encourage education and business startups,	63

ESTATE AND GIFT TAX		
ACTION	RESULT	PAGE
Higher estate tax rate on top 1%	Reduce inequality by increasing vertical equity, encourage descendants to contribute to economy	54

PAYROLL TAXES		
ACTION	RESULT	PAGE
Replace the social security tax with a less regressive tax	Tax consumption, not work, increase vertical equity	11

PROPERTY TAXES		
ACTION	RESULT	PAGE
Equalize property tax rates across each state or across the country	Increased horizontal equity between similar taxpayers in different places	59

CORPORATE INCOME TAX		
ACTION	RESULT	PAGE
Tax foreign income of companies operating in the U.S. when earned	Eliminate opportunity for tax avoidance	30
Tax corporate stock buyback plans as a dividend	Increase horizontal equity by taxing income from buybacks	56
Require or entice states to combine the state corporate income tax with the federal tax	Greatly reduce administrative and compliance costs, reduce opportunities for avoidance	32
Eliminate the corporate income tax	Job and investment growth in the U.S. as companies move back from lower tax countries	32
Restore tax benefits for Employee Stock Ownership Plans (ESOPs)	Decrease inequality by making employees owners of their companies	57

CHARITIES		
ACTION	RESULT	PAGE
Tax charities (property and income)	Eliminate hidden subsidy, reduce tax rates by broadening tax base	52
Eliminate income tax and estate tax deductions for charitable contributions	Eliminate indirect government support for nonprofit organizations	52

POLITICAL SYSTEM CHANGES		
ACTION	RESULT	PAGE
Require disclosure of beneficial owners of all entities in the U.S.	Reduce ability to evade taxes and hide political contributions	59
Block bank transactions with tax haven countries	Reduce ability to evade taxes	59
Require voting by mail nationwide	Reduce discrimination against poor, increased consideration of candidates and proposals	59
Have voting districts set by neutral committees	Eliminate gerrymandering to reduce legislative polarization	59
Federal requirement that state and local governments fully fund pension annual required contributions	Current year taxpayers pay the full future cost of public employee pensions earned during the current year	15
Require all political entities to disclose donors and amounts donated	Publicize donations so as to make obvious the influence of large donors	58
Tax supported child care	Improve work and education ability of parents; encourage business startups, employ childcare workers; improve abilities of future workers	64

Very few people seem satisfied with our current tax system. Perhaps the time has come to get together and see if we can agree on how to fix it. A significant and increasing carbon tax will do much to reduce the impact of climate change on future generations. Broadening the base of the income tax to include nonprofits, eliminating deductions, credits, and exemptions, and taxing all income at the same rates (tax exempt interest, capital gains, employee fringe benefits) would allow tax rates to be drastically reduced. Taxing income (individual and corporate) in the year earned, not when received, and from anywhere in the world, would greatly reduce the perceived unfairness of our tax system.

This would require each of us to forget about the tax breaks we'd personally be losing and instead focus on the benefits to us all of lower tax rates, improved economic efficiency, and increased economic activity.

Increasing the rates of the estate tax and income tax on those at the top and investing those amounts in daycare and preschool for the country would be an investment in our future workforce which would pay back for all of us. It would give parents the chance to complete their educations, start businesses, and contribute to a growing economy. And adopting a VAT, as the rest of the advanced countries in the world have done, would provide more than sufficient funding to invest in significant research, job training, and the infrastructure repairs and investments that could make the U.S. more than able to compete with the world's other quickly growing economies.

These changes won't come quickly or easily, but the resulting value of decreased misery and increased happiness, both today and in the future, assures us that the difficulties are worth overcoming.

BIBLIOGRAPHY

Andrews, Edmund L., "Tax Cuts Offer Most for Very Rich, Study Says", *New York Times,* January 8, 2007

BBC News, "France's 75% tax rate gains approval by top court", 29 December 2013

Brunori, David, *The Future of State Taxation,* (The Urban Press, Washington, D.C., 1998), 198

Bittman, Mark, "Abundance Doesn't Mean Health", *New York Times,* Jan. 21, 2014

Buffett, Warren E., "Stop Coddling the Super-Rich", *New York Times,* August 14, 2011

Burman, Leonard E. and Slemrod, Joel, *Taxes in America,* (New York, Oxford University Press, 2013), 32.

Cardwell, Diane and Krauss, Clifford, "Trucking Industry Is Set to Expand Its Use of Natural Gas", *New York Times*, April 22, 2013

CCH (2014), *Master Tax Guide - Federal, Tax Law Reference Guide*, Wolters Kluwer

Center for Climate and Electricity Policy, *Considering a Carbon Tax: Frequently Asked Questions,* "http://www.rff.org/centers/climate_and_electricity_policy/pages/carbon_tax_faqs.aspx (December 15, 2013)

Charity Navigator, *10 Charities Overpaying their For-Profit Fundraisers*, http://www.charitynavigator.org/index.cfm?bay=topten.detail&listid=28#.UrBMBqW5duY (December 17, 2013)

Confessore, Nicholas and Kocieniewski, David, "For Romneys, Friendly Code Reduces Taxes", *New York Times,* January 24, 2012

Cooper, Michael, "Squeezed Cities Ask Nonprofits for More Money", *New York Times*, May 11, 2011

Davenport, Coral, "Industry Awakens to Threat of Climate Change", *New York Times*, Jan. 23, 2014

Edsal, Thomas B. l, "Whatever Happened to 'Every Man a King'?", *New York Times*, Feb. 11, 2014

Eurostat Statistical Books, "Taxation trends in the European Union", 2013.

Frosch, Dan, "Measures To Legalize Marijuana Are Passed", New York Times, November 6, 2013

Gardiner, Beth, "Is Natural Gas Good, or Just Less Bad"?, *New York Times*, February 22, 2011

Governmental Accounting Standards Board, "Statement 25, Financial Reporting for Defined Benefit Pension Plans and Note Disclosures for Defined Contribution Plans", Norwalk, CT, November 1994

Greene, Joshua (2013), *Moral Tribes: Emotion, Reason, and the Gap Between Us and Them*, Penguin Press

Haisley, Emily, "Loving a bad bet: Factors that induce low-income individuals to purchase state lottery tickets", <http://www.aeaweb.org/annual_mtg_papers/2008/2008_204.pdf>, (December 18, 2013)

Hansell, Saul, "New York State Girds for War With Amazon", *New York Times*, APRIL 14, 2008

Hunt, Albert R., "Do Lower Taxes Create Jobs? Look At Clinton And Bush", *New York Times*, December 16, 2012

Keisling, Phil, "To Enhance Democracy, Expand Vote-by-Mail, Letter to the editor from Phil Keisling, former Oregon secretary of state and chief elections official", *New York Times*, October 20, 2012

Kotlikoff, Laurence J., "Abolish the Corporate Income Tax," *New York Times*, January 5, 2014

Lehrer, Eli, and Sanders, Lori, "Moving to Work", *National Affairs,* Number 18, Winter 2014

Lowrey, Annie, "Switzerland's Proposal to Pay People for Being Alive", *New York Times*, November 12, 2013

Mcintire, Mike and Confessore, Nicholas, "Tax-Exempt Groups Shield Political Gifts of Businesses", *New York Times*, July 7, 2012

Naeem , Waqas, "Nonprofit organizations have become an important part of the U.S. economy", *TimesRecordNews,* Wichita Falls, Texas, May 20, 2012

New York Times, "Voting by Mail", October 6, 2012

Nordfors, Miriam, "Room for Debate: Sweden Solves Two Problems at Once", *New York Times*, February 28, 2013

Norris, Floyd," Economy: Window Is Opening For Change In Tax Code," *New York Times,* Jan. 16, 2014

O'Sullivan, Arthur, Sheffrin Steven M. and Perez, Stephen (2009), *Economics, Principles, Applications and Tools*, Prentice Hall

Organization for Economic Co-operation and Development (OECD), *OECD Better Life Index*, http://www.oecdbetterlifeindex.org/topics/education/ (December 16, 2013)

Organization for Economic Co-operation and Development *Revenue Statistics – Comparative Tables from* http://stats.oecd.org/Index.aspx?DataSetCode=REV (December 30, 2013)

Palmer, Lisa, "Green - Floating Islands to the Rescue", *New York Times*, February 15, 2013

Peterson, David L., U.S. Forest Service forestry research scientist and member of the Intergovernmental Panel on Climate Change (IPCC), e-mail to author, December 14, 2013

Rampell, Catherine, "Value-Added Taxes: A Primer", *New York Times*, April 19, 2010

Randolph, Thomas Jefferson, *Memoir, correspondence, and miscellanies from the papers of Thomas Jefferson Volume III*, (Charlottesville, F. Carr and Co., 1829), 429.

Reich, Rob, "Not Very Giving", *New York Times*, September 4, 2013

Ripley, Amanda, *The Smartest Kids in the World: And How They Got That Way*, (New York, Simon & Schuster, 2013)

Romero, Simon , "Uruguay Acts to Legalize Marijuana", New York Times, December 10, 2013

Roodman, David and Standley, Scott, Center for Global Development, " Working Paper Number 82, Tax policies to promote private charitable giving in DAC countries", (January 2006), page 15

Saez, Emmanuel, *Striking it Richer: The Evolution of Top Incomes in the United States*, http://elsa.berkeley.edu/~saez/saez-UStopincomes-2012.pdf (December 15, 2013)

Samuelson, Paul and Nordhaus, William (2009), *Economics,* McGraw Hill/Irwin

Sandford, Cedric, *Why Tax Systems Differ,* (Fiscal Publications, Bath, England, 2000)

Shabecoff, Philip, "E.P.A. Orders 90 Percent Cut In Lead Content Of Gasoline By 1986", *New York Times,* March 5, 1985

Smith, Adam, *An Inquiry into the Nature and Causes of the Wealth of Nations Vol. II, 2nd edition,* (London, W. Strahan and T. Cadell 1778), 425

Rattner, Steven, "America in 2013, as Told in Charts," *New York Times,* December 30, 2013

Schwartz, John, "Small Infrastructure Gains Are Observed in Engineering Report", *New York Times,* March 19, 2013

Stiglitz, Joseph E. (2012), *The Price of Inequality: How Today's Divided Society Endangers Our Future,* Norton

Thaler, Richard H. and Sunstein, Cass R. (2009), *Nudge: Improving Decisions About Health, Wealth, and Happiness,* Penguin Books

The case of Gregory v. Helvering 69 F.2d 809, 810 (2d Cir. 1934), aff'd, 293 U.S. 465, 55 S.Ct. 266, 79 L.Ed. 596 (1935)

The Council of Economic Advisers, "Supporting Research and Development to Promote Economic Growth: The Federal Government's Role", October 1995

The Economist, "Free Exchange - All men are created unequal", January 4, 2014, 60

The Economist, "Going public, and private – Health care in America", December 21, 2013.

The Economist, "Mulled Whines – Alcohol Pricing", Dec. 21, 2013, 99.

The Economist, "Carbon Copy - Companies and emissions", December 14, 2013

The Economist, "Unemployment – Long time gone", Jan. 4, 2014, 19.

Thuronyi, Victor, *Comparative Tax Law,* (Kluwer Law International, The Hague, The Netherlands, 2003

Velasquez-Manoff, Moises, "The Great Divide: What Happens When The Poor Receive A Stipend?", *New York Times,* January 18, 2014

Villega, Paulina, "Mexico: Junk Food Tax Is Approved," *New York Times*, October 31, 2013

Wang, Sam, "The Great Gerrymander of 2012", *New York Times*, February 2, 2013

Weiss, Ann E., Lotteries, *Who Wins, Who Loses?*, (Hillside, N.J., Enslow, 1991), 65

Wikipedia article "Carbon Tax"

Wikipedia page "California Proposition 13"

World Bank Indicators "GDP per capita by year and country in 2013 U.S. dollars adjusted for inflation" from http://data.worldbank.org/indicator/NY.GDP.MKTP.CD (December 13, 2013)

Wyatt, Edward, "U.S. Struggles to Keep Pace in Delivering Broadband Service," *New York Times*, December 29, 2013

TAX DICTIONARY

abated Reduced an amount.

accelerated depreciation results in a greater expense than straight line in each early year, offset by a lower expense in each later year. MACRS depreciation used for income tax purposes allows 200% declining balance and 150% declining balance depreciation methods for certain assets.

accountable plan A plan to reimburse an employee for business expenses incurred only if substantiated.

accrual basis When the accrual basis is used for an income tax return, income is reported when earned, whether or not it has been actually or constructively received. Deductions and credits are allowed in the year they are accrued or incurred. The accrual basis must be used where inventories are necessary.

accumulated earnings and profits is used to find the tax on excess accumulated earnings. It is the sum of total current earnings and profits for all tax years but the present year less any deficit in current earnings and profits for prior tax years. Distributions (dividends) to shareholders first reduce current earnings and then reduce accumulated earnings from prior years.

accumulated earnings tax If a corporation accumulates more than a reasonable amount of retained earnings (to avoid dividends taxable to owners), a tax is imposed on the excess. A reasonable amount depends on the needs of the corporation. Up to $250,000 can be accumulated by most corporations without justification of corporate need.

ace "adjusted current earnings" is the alternative minimum taxable income (before the ACE preference or NOL deduction) adjusted for depreciation allowances, exclusions from gross income, and certain deductions and special items.

acquisition mortgage Up to $1,000,000 of debt, secured by the property, incurred to buy, build, or substantially improve a qualified residence.

adjusted basis of property is cost plus the cost of improvements, purchase commissions, and other costs such as recording and appraisal fees. This is reduced by depreciation allowed or allowable for income tax purposes.

aggregate The total or gross amount.

AGI An individual's AGI (Adjusted Gross Income) is found by subtracting deductions allowed from gross income. These deductions include business expenses (but not employee business expenses), penalties for early savings withdrawal, contributions to self-employed retirement plans, IRA contributions, alimony, expenses incurred in producing rent or royalty income, moving expenses, and contributions to medical savings plans.

aging of accounts receivable is a listing of accounts by the length of time the receivables have been outstanding. A larger percentage of older accounts are estimated uncollectible than accounts from more recent sales.

alimony payments are made to a former spouse under a divorce or separation instrument. To be deducted by the payer, alimony can't be described in the decree as property settlement or as child support. Alimony may not extend beyond the death of the payee, and the former spouses may not live in the same household.

alternative depreciation system (ADS) MACRS depreciation for income tax purposes is actually two systems. The most commonly used is the general depreciation system (GDS). The other, the alternative depreciation system (ADS), must be used for certain types of property and taxpayers may choose to use it for others. ADS depreciation is usually over a longer period and is only straight line.

alternative fuel production credit A producer may claim a nonrefundable income tax credit for domestic production and sale of oil, gas, and synthetic fuels from nonconventional sources.

amend To change. A tax return previously filed is amended by filing a form 1040X (individuals) or 1120X (corporations).

amortizable An amount that can be amortized by expensing it over a time longer than one year. Bond premium or discount is amortized over the life of the bonds.

amt (amti) The alternative minimum tax (AMT) insures that all higher income taxpayers pay at least a minimum income tax. To find the tax, regular taxable income is increased by tax preferences and adjustments, then reduced by an exemption. That gives the alternative minimum taxable income (AMTI). Multiplying the AMTI by the alternative minimum tax rate gives the tentative alternative minimum tax. The alternative minimum tax paid is the tentative tax less the regular income tax.

annualized income A method for determining required estimated tax payments by basing estimated tax payments on taxable income earned each quarter of the year.

annuity An investment on which one receives fixed payments each year for a specified number of years.

applicable credit The federal estate tax is imposed on the "taxable estate" at death. The gross estate includes taxable lifetime gifts. The gross estate tax is found by multiplying the taxable estate (the gross estate less deductions) by the estate tax rates. The applicable credit is subtracted from the gross estate tax.

appreciated Increased in value over time.

assess (assessment) The IRS assesses past due taxes as part of the collection process. To assess for property tax purposes is to value or appraise the property. The assessed amount is the appraised amount on which the property tax is based.

assumed A party who was not liable on a debt "assumed" an existing debt when that party become personally liable on the debt.

basis The amount subtracted from value received to determine gain or loss. Usually the cost of the asset sold or exchanged. Sometimes called "adjusted basis" when cost is increased or decreased to determine a new basis.

beneficiary The recipient of funds from a life insurance policy or an estate.

bequest (bequeathed) Leave property by a will.

book income is income before income taxes for financial reporting purposes.

business expenses are deductible if ordinary and necessary for a trade or business conducted by the taxpayer, and paid or incurred during the tax year in which deducted.

c corporation For income tax purposes there are two types of corporations. S corporation income is taxed only to the shareholders and not to the corporation. The income of C corporations is taxed twice, first to the corporation and again to the shareholders as dividends.

calendar year January 1 to December 31.

capital A partner's capital account is the equity of that partner in the partnership. The total of all partners' capital accounts equals total assets less total liabilities.

capital asset For income tax purposes, capital assets include investments and property not acquired for production of income.

capital gain is gain on the sale or exchange of a capital asset.

capital loss is loss on the sale or exchange of a capital asset.

carryback Taxpayers who have a negative taxable income (net operating loss, NOL) because expenses exceed revenue, can carry that loss back or forward. They can offset it against positive taxable income of the other years and recompute the tax of the other year on the smaller taxable income. The NOL results in a refund of excess tax paid in the prior year and reduction of tax due in future years.

cash basis When the cash basis is used for an income tax return, income is reported when received (or earlier if the taxpayer had the power to receive it but chose not to). Most deductions and credits are allowed in the year paid. Most individuals are cash basis taxpayers. The accrual basis must be used where inventories are necessary.

casualty Losses to property are deductible as casualty losses if they result from fire, storm, shipwreck, or other casualty (unexpected, accidental force exerted on property where the taxpayer is powerless to prevent it). Taxpayers sometime receive insurance payments above the income tax basis of property, resulting in casualty gains.

charitable contributions Individuals who itemize and corporations are allowed to deduct contributions to charitable, religious, educational and scientific organizations, or government units in the United States.

child and dependent care credit Individuals are allowed a credit for work related expenses paid for the care of children and dependents who are incapable of self-care.

child support Payments specified by a divorce decree for the support of a minor child are not deductible by the payer and are not income to the recipient.

civil fraud penalty is 75% of any tax underpayment attributed to fraud. It is a monetary penalty, separate from criminal charges against taxpayers who file fraudulent returns.

collateral The goods covered by a security interest to secure repayment of a debt. If scheduled payments are not made, the creditor can take possession of collateral, sell it, and use the proceeds to pay the secured debt.

consolidated tax return A combined income tax return for a chain of corporations connected through stock ownership with a common parent.

constant yield to maturity A method of amortizing interest. The effective yield on the principal is multiplied by the outstanding balance at the beginning of each period to determine interest income or expense that period. Premium or discount is amortized so that interest expense or income equals that amount.

constructively Income is constructively received by a taxpayer (included in income) when credited to his account, set apart for him, or available so he may draw on it at any time, or could have if he had given notice of intention.

corporate charter The document issued by a state creating a corporation.

corpus The principal or capital of a trust or estate as distinguished from income earned.

credit for the elderly or disabled An income tax credit for those aged 65 or older and those with permanent and total disability.

credits Unlike deductions, income tax credits are subtracted directly from the total tax. Some are refundable (the IRS will write the taxpayer a check) and others are nonrefundable (no check to the taxpayer).

current earnings and profits Taxable income plus excluded items such as tax exempt interest income less excess charitable contributions.

death benefit Amount paid to family or estate of a deceased employee by the employer.

decedent A dead person.

declining-balance An accelerated depreciation method. For example, with 200% declining balance depreciation, depreciation expense each year is found by multiplying (2 divided by the useful life) times book value. Book value is cost less accumulated depreciation, so each year's depreciation is smaller than that of the previous year.

deductible (deductibility) An expense or loss is deductible if it can be subtracted from revenue to find taxable income, thus reducing income tax.

deemed distribution A prohibited transaction, such as a loan to the owner by a retirement account, is treated as an early distribution from the account. It is taxable in that year and is subject to the penalty for early withdrawal from tax deferred retirement accounts.

deferred in general means past cash receipts and payments related to future events, so revenue or expense is recognized in a period later than the receipt or payment of the cash. Deferred gross profit under the installment sales method of revenue recognition is the gross profit not yet recognized at a given date.

delinquency penalty A nondeductible penalty for late payment of taxes.

delinquent Overdue in payment.

deposits Tax deposits are payments of tax to the account of the U. S. Treasury.

disabled access credit A credit for small businesses for expenditures to make the business accessible to disabled individuals.

disbursements Cash payments.

distribution Cash or property transferred by a business to its owners. Partners receive partnership distributions. Shareholders receive corporate distributions. A liquidating distribution is a return of the capital invested. A nonliquidating distribution is income on that investment.

dividend Cash or property transferred by a corporation to its shareholders.

dividends received deduction (exclusion) A corporation that receives a dividend from another corporation that has paid the U.S. corporate income tax can deduct (exclude) a percentage and pay income tax on only the remaining amount. The deduction varies between 70%, 80%, and 100% based on the percentage of the other company's shares owned. This reduces the effect of multiple taxation on the income, which has been taxed to the first corporation, is taxed again to the receiving corporation, and is taxed yet again to the individual who owns shares in the receiving corporation.

dni "distributable net income" is the accounting income of an estate or trust. There are no deductions for distributions to beneficiaries, personal exemptions, and capital losses (unless these were offset against distributable gains). To that amount is added tax exempt interest not allocable to trust disbursements.

domestic Within the United States.

draw (drawing) Distribution of income to partners by a partnership.

earned income credit is found by multiplying an individual's earned income by a percentage. It is a refundable income tax credit available to individuals with AGI below certain limits.

earnings and profits Accumulated earnings and profits is used to find the tax on excess accumulated earnings. It is the sum of current earnings and profits for all tax years but the present year less deficits in current earnings and profits for prior tax years. Dividends to shareholders first reduce current earnings and profits.

esa An education savings account similar to an IRA.

elect (election) A taxpayer makes an election by choosing between acceptable alternatives. For example, a taxpayer can elect not to carry NOLs back, but to carry them forward instead.

enhanced oil recovery credit A credit for beginning or expanding a domestic oil recovery project that uses a tertiary recovery method to increase the amount of crude oil recovered.

estate The possessions and debts left by a person at death.

estate income tax The income tax paid by an estate on its income.

estate tax Federal gift and estate taxes are imposed on the value of property transferred. The estate tax is based on the value of an individual's property at death.

estimated income tax laws require that taxpayers make payments during the tax year of the estimated tax due for that year instead of paying the tax in one lump sum after year end.

exclude (exclusion) An amount not included in income or the value of a gift or estate.

executor A person appointed by a testator to execute the testator's will.

exempt organization To be exempt from income tax, organizations must fall into one of the specific classes permitted. They file information returns (except churches). They are only taxed (at corporate rates) on net income from unrelated business activities above $1,000. The classes of exempt organizations are religious, charitable, scientific, testing for public safety, literary, educational, national or international sports competition, prevention of cruelty to children or animals, political organizations, civic leagues, and social clubs.

exemptions Individuals are entitled to a personal exemption and to dependency exemptions on their income tax returns. Taxpayers liable for the AMT are entitled to an alternative minimum tax exemption.

extension payment is a payment of tax with the extension form sent to the IRS requesting additional time to file the tax return.

extension request is a formal request to the IRS for additional time to file a tax return.

fiscal period A reporting time period other than the calendar year.

foreign corporation A corporation organized outside the U.S. Foreign corporations are liable for U.S. taxes on U.S. income.

foreign tax credit The U.S. imposes an income tax on income from foreign sources. To minimize double taxation of the same income, a foreign tax credit is allowed against the U.S. income tax for foreign income tax paid on income that is also taxed in the U.S.

forfeiture Something surrendered as a penalty.

franchise tax A tax imposed on business operations in a given geographic area.

fraud The civil fraud penalty is 75% of the portion of any tax underpayment attributed to fraud. It is a monetary penalty, separate from criminal charges against taxpayers who file fraudulent returns.

future interest A gift in trust is a gift of a present interest if the trust will receive income, some portion of that income will flow steadily to beneficiaries, and the portion of the income flowing to beneficiaries can be ascertained. Other gifts in trust are future interests.

gain is the excess of the sales price of an asset over its adjusted basis.

general business credit A single credit combining the investment tax credit, rehabilitation credit, energy credit, reforestation credit, work opportunity credit, alcohol fuels credit, research credit, low income housing credit, enhanced oil recovery credit, disabled access credit, renewable electricity production credit, empowerment zone credit, Indian employment credit, orphan drug credit, and the employer social security credit.

general liability A debt for which the partners of the partnership have unlimited liability.

generation skipping transfer tax Wealthy individuals could avoid the estate tax paid by their children by giving assets instead to grandchildren or great grandchildren directly. The generation skipping transfer tax is imposed in addition to any gift or estate tax due.

gift tax Federal gift and estate taxes are imposed on the value of property transferred. The estate tax is based on the value of an individual's property at death. Wealthy people could escape estate tax by making gifts while they are alive, so a similar tax is imposed on the value of gifts from one living individual to another.

grantor trust A person (the grantor) who transfers property to a trust and retains powers or interests is treated as the owner of the trust for income tax purposes.

gross estate The value of a decedent's assets at death.

gross income For income tax purposes, gross income is any value received (cash, real property, personal property, or services) unless it is a gift, something already owned by the taxpayer, or an exclusion from income.

gross receipts The gross sales revenue of a business. Returns and allowances are subtracted from gross receipts to find net sales. Cost of sales is subtracted from net sales to find gross profit.

group medical policy A plan that provides insurance for the medical care of a group of employees.

guaranteed payments are fixed or guaranteed amounts paid by a partnership to its partners for services or the use of capital. Guaranteed payments are taxable income to the partner and are a business deduction to the partnership.

half-year convention The half year convention is used to compute depreciation for income tax purposes for all property other than nonresidential real and residential rental property. Property is assumed to have been placed in service or disposed of in the middle of the year. Half of the first year's depreciation is allowed the year the property is placed in service and a half year's depreciation is allowed for the year when the property is retired.

health savings account A tax deductible savings plan that may only be used for medical costs.

heir One who inherits property under a will.

home-equity Up to $100,000 of debt, secured by the taxpayer's residence, incurred for any reason other than to buy, build, or substantially improve the residence.

inclusion An amount included in gross income for income tax purposes.

incorporating Creating a new corporation.

individual retirement account An IRA is a retirement account set up in the name of an individual taxpayer on which income tax is deferred until payments are made to the taxpayer after retirement. Higher income taxpayers covered by a qualified pension plan can make contributions to an IRA that are not currently deductible. Contributions to a "Roth IRA" are not deductible, but income is distributed tax-free.

infringement An invasion of the rights of another.

inheritance Property received as a bequest in a will.

inter-vivos Between living people.

intercompany Balances and transactions between companies within a group of companies under common control.

intracompany Within one company.

investment company Regulated investment companies escape income tax if they pass the income to their shareholders, who then pay tax on that income.

investment interest Individual taxpayers can deduct interest paid on loans that are invested in investments that produce taxable income. The expense deduction is limited to the amount of net investment income.

irs Internal Revenue Service.

itemized Individual taxpayers can claim itemized deductions in determining taxable income for medical expenses, state and local taxes, charitable contributions, some interest, casualty and theft losses, and miscellaneous itemized deductions.

joint income tax return Married individuals can elect to file one joint income tax return instead of each filing their own separate return.

k-1 Schedule K-1 is attached to a partnership or S corporation income tax return. It shows the allocation of various types of income to the partners or shareholders.

lessee A person who holds a right to use property under a lease.

lessor One who leases property to another.

lien The right to sell property of a debtor as security for payment of a debt.

life insurance premium The cost of purchasing a life insurance policy.

limited partnership A partnership with some partners who have their personal liability for partnership debts limited to their investment.

liquidate (liquidation) To convert other assets into cash.

liquidating dividends are dividends paid above income earned. Not taxed as income on the investment, but treated as a return of capital invested.

long-term capital gain A gain realized on sale or disposal of a capital asset held over twelve months.

loss is the excess of the adjusted basis of an asset over its sales price.

macrs depreciation used for income tax purposes is actually two systems. The most commonly used is the general depreciation system (GDS), which allows 200% declining balance and 150% declining balance depreciation methods. The other, the alternative depreciation system (ADS), must be used for certain types of property and taxpayers may choose to use it for others. Depreciation under ADS is only straight line.

marginal tax rate is the rate of tax on the last dollar earned, which doesn't change the lower tax rate on the first few dollars of income.

medical expenses for the taxpayer, spouse, or dependent are deducted as an itemized deduction if paid or charged to a credit card during the tax year. They must be for diagnosis, cure, treatment, mitigation, or prevention of disease, treatment affecting bodily function or structure, transportation costs essential for medical care, medical insurance, lodging incidental to care away from home, or for prescription drugs or insulin. Only medical expenses above 7.5% of AGI are deducted as an itemized deduction.

mid-month convention is used for straight line depreciation of real property. The deduction is based on the number of months the property was in service, with half of a month allowed for the months of acquisition and disposal.

minimum tax credit The alternative minimum tax insures that all taxpayers with income pay at least a minimum income tax. To find the tax, regular taxable income is increased by tax preferences and adjustments, then reduced by an exemption amount, sometimes called the minimum tax credit. That gives the alternative minimum taxable income (AMTI). Multiplying the AMTI by the alternative minimum tax rate gives the tentative alternative minimum tax. The tentative tax is paid if it exceeds the regular income tax.

miscellaneous itemized deductions include expenses of tax returns or tax advice, expenses incurred in production of income (other than business, rent, and royalty), unreimbursed employee business expenses, professional and union dues, employee education expenses, cost of seeking a new job in the same profession, investment expenses, hobby losses not to exceed hobby income, gambling losses not to exceed winnings, and expenses incurred in producing income in respect of a decedent.

modified AGI is used to determine the amount of social security benefits to be included in gross income. Modified AGI is AGI without social security benefits plus tax exempt interest earned plus the exclusion for U.S. citizens living abroad, plus excluded income from possessions of the U.S., plus excluded interest from U.S. savings bonds used for higher education costs.

monies Plural of money.

mortgage Right to sell another's land (foreclose) as security for a debt.

municipal bond Interest earned on a bond issued by a state or political subdivision (a municipal bond) for essential government functions is excluded from income.

net operating loss If a taxpayer has a negative taxable income (expenses minus revenue equals the net operating loss, NOL) they can carry that loss back, offset it against positive taxable income of prior years, and recompute the tax on the smaller taxable income. The IRS will refund excess tax paid in the prior year. A taxpayer can also carry NOLs forward and subtract the NOL from the positive taxable incomes of future years to reduce income tax paid in those years.

noncapital Not a capital asset or a capital expenditure.

nonexempt Not exempt from taxation.

nonfraudulent Not involving fraud. Fraud is a false representation intended to deceive relied on by another to that person's injury.

nonliquidating A distribution to owners from earnings is a distribution of income, so it is not a liquidating distribution. Distributions in excess of earnings are liquidating distributions, a return of capital invested.

nonresidential Not used for residential (a place where people dwell) purposes.

omission To fail to include or leave out.

ordinary gain A gain taxed at ordinary income rates as opposed to long-term capital gain rates.

ordinary income is the net income and expense not reported separately to partners. Items taxed differently on the income tax returns of various partners, such as long-term capital gains and charitable contributions, are not included in ordinary income.

organizational costs (organization expense) are the costs of creating a business. A new business can deduct the first $5,000 and amortize the remaining organization costs straight line over 180 months. Organization costs include legal and accounting fees incurred as part of organizing the business, and filing fees.

outside salesperson A person occupied in making sales calls outside the employer's place of business.

paid-in capital is contributed by owners as opposed to earnings retained in the business.

partnership interest A partner's share of a partnership. The capital of a business is its owners' equity, (total assets less liabilities). In a partnership, each partner has a capital account. The total of these accounts is the owners' equity of the partnership.

passive losses are not deducted from nonpassive income. Passive sources are businesses with no material direct participation by this owner or rentals (regardless of participation). Portfolio income (dividends and interest) is not included in this definition of passive income.

penalty A nondeductible charge for late payment of taxes. The IRS imposes penalties on tax preparers who fail to sign a return or fail to provide the taxpayer with a copy. The IRS also imposes penalties on tax preparers who negotiate a client's refund check. IRS penalties are not assessed for simple errors in calculations.

percentage depletion is an expense deducted to compute taxable income equal to a percentage of the income (receipts) produced by mineral property. It is not limited by the cost of the mineral property.

personal exemption Individuals are entitled to a personal exemption for themselves and another for their spouse. They are also entitled to dependency exemptions for each dependent claimed on their income tax return.

personal property In law, moveable property (not land). In tax personal property means any property used for personal (not income producing) purposes.

phase out To bring something to an end, one step at a time.

preceding year method An individual can escape the underpayment penalty for estimated taxes by paying estimated taxes for the current year equal to 100% of the prior year liability.

preferences Alternative minimum tax preferences include accelerated depreciation, mining exploration and development costs, the completed contract method, amortization of pollution control facilities, the installment method, the net operating loss deduction, and certain losses.

premium on issuance of a bond or note is the excess of the issue price over face value.

preparer is someone who prepares a tax return.

present interest In a gift of a present interest the donee has an unrestricted right to immediate use, possession or enjoyment of the property or the income from that property.

private activity bonds are bonds issued by a government to finance nongovernment activities, such as the development of an industrial park or to fund student loans.

private foundation Any exempt organization other than one with broad public support

public charity (public service charitable organization) Exempt organizations that receive at least one third of support from governments and the general public, or at least 10% of their support from the public and governments and are organized so as to attract new and additional public support. The important distinction is between a public charity (not taxed) and a private foundation (subject to taxes).

qualified charitable organization Contributions can be deducted only if they are made to eligible organizations. The IRS lists all eligible organizations in Publication 78, which determines whether an organization qualifies.

qualified education expenses To be deductible, an employee's education expenses must maintain or improve skills required in current employment. Educational costs that qualify a person for a different job or meet minimum qualifications of the present job are not deductible.

qualified pension plan A tax deferred retirement plan. Contributions made by the employer are currently deductible. The income is not taxed until benefits are paid to the employee after retirement.

qualified residence interest An itemized deduction for interest paid on loans secured by the taxpayer's first or second home. It includes both mortgages (where the proceeds of the loan was used to build, buy, or improve the residence) and home equity loans (loans secured by title to the residence where the proceeds were used for any other purpose).

qualified widow(er) When a taxpayer dies, the surviving spouse files a joint return for that year. The widow(er) files as a qualifying widow(er) using the joint rates during the next two years if he/she remains unmarried and has a dependent child living with him/her.

qualifying business meals qualify for a business deduction while out of town on business overnight. The deduction is 50% of the amount spent.

qualifying reorganization A qualifying reorganization (no gain or loss to stockholders or the corporations) is one of these: 1. A statutory merger or consolidation. 2. The acquisition of a controlling stock interest in another corporation solely for voting stock of the acquiring corporation. 3. The acquisition of substantially all property of another corporation solely for voting stock of the acquiring corporation. 4. Transfer by a corporation of all or part of its assets to another corporation if immediately afterwards the transferor or its shareholders control the corporation to which the assets are transferred. 5. A recapitalization. 6. A mere change in identity, form, or place of organization. 7. A transfer by a corporation in bankruptcy.

real property Land and anything permanently attached to the land (a fixture).

realized Gains or losses for income tax purposes are realized when a taxpayer converts property (real or personal, tangible or intangible) into other property or cash. Exchanges are bargained transactions where each party gives and receives something as opposed to one-sided transactions such as death benefits or gifts. Gain or loss is found by subtracting the adjusted basis from the amount realized in the exchange. Amount realized is the cash received, plus fair market value of other property received, plus any seller liabilities to be paid by the buyer.

recapture Retaking or recovering an amount. Some income tax deductions and credits are recaptured in a later year, requiring the taxpayer to pay then to the IRS some of tax saved in the earlier year.

recognized Gain or loss realized is recognized for income tax purposes when it increases or decreases the income tax of a year.

refund of tax is a payment by the IRS to the taxpayer of amounts paid to the IRS above that owed.

regular tax is the income tax as opposed to the alternative minimum tax.

regulated investment companies escape income tax if they pass income to shareholders.

reimbursement (reimburse) To repay money spent. An employer reimburses an employee for business expenses incurred by the employee.

remainder interest Something left over after other parts have been taken. The remainder interest in a trust is the balance left after income is distributed to income beneficiaries.

s corporation A corporation that meets certain requirements can elect to be taxed as a partnership. Income is taxed to the stockholders when earned rather than when distributed; capital gains or losses and other items that receive special treatment on an individual return are passed through to the stockholders separately from ordinary income.

schedule A is the schedule attached to an individual income tax return that lists itemized deductions.

self-employment tax (self-employment income) A tax is imposed on income earned by self-employed individuals in a trade or business. The tax is for social security and Medicare. Individuals who pay the self-employment tax can deduct 50% of the tax paid from gross income in computing AGI.

series ee bonds Interest earned on series EE U.S. savings bonds is excluded from income if the proceeds of the bond are used to pay for higher education expenses of the taxpayer, the spouse, or dependents.

simplified employee pension plan In a SEP the employer makes contributions to the IRA of each employee, which are deductible in the year made. The employee is not taxed until benefits are paid to the employee after retirement.

social security benefits FICA (Federal Insurance Contributions Act or social security), pays old age, survivors, and disability benefits to eligible individuals. These benefits are taxed to higher income individuals.

sole proprietor An individual who owns 100% of an unincorporated business.

special deductions on a corporate income tax return include the dividends received deduction and some other unusual items.

standard deduction A deduction allowed on the income tax return of an individual instead of itemized deductions. The larger of the standard deduction or total itemized deductions is taken.

statute of limitations The general statute of limitations for tax returns is three years. A taxpayer can usually not amend a return after three years, and the IRS can usually not impose additional taxes more than three years after the return is filed.

stock dividend A dividend of shares of stock in the distributing company.

straight-line Amortization or depreciation of an asset by an equal expense each year.

subsidiary A company having more than half of its stock owned by another company.

substantiated Supported with proof or evidence.

tax exempt Interest earned on a bond issued by a state or political subdivision (a municipal bond) to finance essential government functions is excluded from income tax. An exempt organization is an organization such as a church that does not pay income tax.

tax liability The amount of tax owed to the IRS.

tax year The time period for which a tax return is filed. Individuals use the calendar year. When a new business is started it often has a short tax year of less than 12 months, starting the day the business is formed and ending December 31 of that year. A fiscal year is a year that ends on a date other than December 31.

taxable estate is the amount on which the estate tax is imposed at death. The gross estate tax is found by multiplying the taxable estate (the gross estate less deductions and the applicable exemption) by estate tax rates.

taxable income Corporate taxable income is found by adding taxable gains to revenue and deducting business expenses, NOL deductions, the dividend received deduction, deductible charitable contributions, and deductible losses. An individual's taxable income is found by starting with gross income, then subtracting deductions to arrive at AGI, subtracting exemptions and subtracting the greater of the standard deduction or total itemized deductions.

tentative minimum tax The alternative minimum tax insures that all higher income taxpayers pay at least a minimum income tax. To find the tax, regular taxable income is increased by tax preferences and adjustments, then reduced by an exemption amount. That gives the alternative minimum taxable income (AMTI). Multiplying the AMTI by the alternative minimum tax rate gives the tentative alternative minimum tax. The tentative tax is paid if it exceeds the regular income tax.

term life insurance is an insurance policy that pays the policy amount if the covered individual dies during a specific time period.

termination A partnership terminates for income tax purposes if its operations are discontinued and no part of its business, financial operation, or venture continues to be carried on by any of its partners in a partnership form.

testator A person who writes a will.

threshold A point of beginning. For income tax purposes some expenses are deductible only above a threshold, such as medical expenses above 7.5% of AGI and casualty losses above 10% of AGI.

timely Within the required time period.

type b reorganization A reorganization (without gain or loss to stockholders or the corporations) that is the acquisition of a controlling stock interest in another corporation solely for voting stock of the acquiring corporation.

unaffiliated Not a member of a group of corporations under common control.

unappreciated An asset that has not increased in value over time.

unemployment compensation benefits are payments to an unemployed individual.

unencumbered Property that is not pledged as security for a loan.

uniform capitalization An income tax rule that requires business taxpayers to capitalize direct costs and an allocable portion of indirect costs attributable to property produced or acquired for resale. Since the costs are capitalized and carried forward as an asset until the year sold, the costs are not currently deducted. The effect is to increase income tax currently due.

unrealized In general, not yet collected, sold, or taxed. If investments have not been sold then no gain has been realized or taxed. Unrealized receivables in a sale of a cash basis partnership have not yet been taxed and are allocated to the partners, then taxed as ordinary income. Interest income is unrealized if it has been earned but not yet collected.

unreimbursed Reimbursement is to repay money spent. An employer reimburses an employee for business expenses incurred. Unreimbursed expenses are expenses for which the employee is not reimbursed.

unrelated business income Exempt organizations pay income tax on business income not related to their exempt function. This is to prevent exempt organizations from unfairly competing with businesses that are taxed.

unrelated business taxable income The gross income derived by an exempt organization from unrelated trade or business regularly carried on by it, less exemptions and allowable deductions. The unrelated business taxable income is taxed at corporate income tax rates.

valuation date The estate tax is based on the value of the estate at the date of death. The alternative valuation date is six months after death. The valuation date selected is also the date on which the value passes to an heir to determine gain or loss on later sale.

vested An immediate right to future benefit. An employee has a vested pension right if the employee has the right to receive the pension even if the employee quits the job.

withheld The amount kept back. Employers are required to withhold income tax.

INDEX

ability to collect the tax, 5

ability to pay principle, 4

accretion concept, 22

adjusted gross income, 22

agricultural fertilizers, 10

air travel, 48

alcohol, 9

alternative minimum tax, 33

annual exclusion, 36

applicable credit, 36

apprenticeship programs, 46

austerity, 45

Australia, 46

Austria, 54

authorization for spending, 2

beneficial owners, 59

benefit principle, 3

Bentham, Jeremy, 43

British Columbia, 9

broad band Internet, 50

Buffet, Warren, 55

burden of taxation, 29

Bush, George W., 45

California, 14

capital assets, 23

capital gains, 23

carbon emission pricing, 47

carbon emissions, 47, 62

carbon tax, 62

casinos, 40

casualty or theft losses, 25

changes to consider, 66

changing the system, 7

charitable contributions, 52

charities, 52

charity ranking, 53

child care, 64

Chile., 46

China, 50

classes on the Internet, 65

Clinton, Bill, 45

Colbert, Jean Baptiste, 2

colleges and universities, 65

Colorado, 10

compliance cost, 5

conservatives, 63

consumption taxes, 19

contributions, 25

control over taxes, 2

corporate income tax, 6, 30

cost of collection, 5

costs of compliance, 62

costs of health care, 10

C-type corporations, 30

current tax system, 7

customs duties, 9

deductible taxes, 24

deductions, 22

deflation, 39

Delta Airlines, 47

Denmark, 18, 46, 54

dependent, 25

depletion expense, 30

dividends, 26

dividends from C-type corporations, 51

dumping, 11

earned income credit, 26

education, 45, 65

Educational Savings Accounts, 23

elderly population, 19

eliminating income tax returns, 62

employee fringe benefits, 61

Employee Stock Ownership Plans (ESOPs), 57

enforcement, 8

EPA, 1

equitable taxation, 3

estate tax, 35, 58

estate tax credits, 37

Europe, 50

evasion, 26

excise tax on carbon, 48

excise taxes, 9

exclusions, 22

exempt organizations, 33

externalities, 29

Exxon Mobile, 47

financial wizards, 46

Finland, 46, 54

fire department, 1

foreign competition, 11

foreign subsidiaries, 47
forgiveness of debt, 23
France, 56
fringe benefits, 23
GASB, 14
generation skipping transfer tax, 37
generation-skipping tax, 35
Germany, 46
gerrymandering, 59
gift tax, 35
global warming, 47, 62
government owned businesses, 40
Great Britain, 62
gross income, 23
guaranteed income, 64
health spending, 10
hidden subsidies, 41
hidden tax, 39
high speed rail, 50
historical view, 2
horizontal equity, 4, 21, 51
immigrants, 63
import bans or quotas, 11
import duties, 11

imported goods, 62
incentives to businesses, 17
incidence of taxation, 4
indirect taxes, 39
individual income tax, 21
inequality, 54
inflation, 39
inflation-protected bonds, 40
infrastructure, 49
inherited property, 37
interest, 25
Interstate Highway system, 56
itemized deductions, 24
Japan, 50
Jefferson, Thomas, 40
liberals, 64
Life insurance proceeds, 23
long term capital gains, 26, 51
lotteries, 40
lower tax rates, 55
mail ballots, 59
major donors, 59
marijuana, 10
maximum estate tax rate, 56

medical expenses, 24

Medicare benefits, 11

Medicare contribution tax, 26

Mexico, 10, 63

military, 1

Mill, John Stuart, 43

minimum income, 63

NAFTA, 11

natural gas, 49

negative attitude toward taxes, 62

New Hampshire, 17

nexus, 18

nonprofit organizations, 51

Norway, 54

objectives of taxation, 2

Oregon, 17, 59

partnerships, 30

pensions, 14

percentage depletion, 30, 51

personal exemption, 25

Peterson, David L., 48

Poland), 46

political influence, 57

preschools, 64

productivity, 54

progressive tax rates, 4

property tax, 13

property tax bill, 2

property tax rates, 57

proportional tax, 4

Proposition 13, 14

public services, 2

realized, 22

regressive tax rates, 4

research, 50

retirement plan contributions, 24

right wing news outlets, 58

risk of inflation, 40

Romney, Mitt, 55

Roth IRAs, 23

sales taxes, 4, 6, 17

sales taxes,, 17

savers, 40

scholarship or fellowship grants, 23

share buyback plans, 31, 56

Shell, 47

sin taxes, 9

Smith, Adam, 3

social security (FICA), 11
social security benefits, 23
social security tax, 5
social welfare programs, 63
sports culture, 47
standard deduction, 24
state corporate income tax, 32
state income tax, 21
stealth taxes, 40
stepped-up basis, 31, 37
stock options, 31
S-type corporations, 30
Sweden, 44, 46, 54, 64
Swiss bank accounts, 6
Switzerland, 15, 63
tax avoidance, 6
tax equity, 27
tax evasion, 6
tax expenditures, 42, 62
tax gap, 8

tax preferences, 33
teachers, 46
tobacco, 9
tobacco taxes, 5
transfer tax, 35
unemployment, 63
unemployment benefits, 23
Uruguay, 10
utilitarians, 43
value added taxes, 18
VAT, 61
vertical equity, 4, 21
Washington, 10, 17, 59
Wealth of Nations, 3
wealth tax, 15
wealthy taxpayers, 56
welfare benefits, 23
Why we have governments, 1
withholding, 26

ABOUT THE AUTHOR

Al Francisco has spent his career teaching classes and writing books for people studying for the CPA exam, first at Idaho State University, then around the U.S. He learned that many people, even those studying for the CPA exam, know very little about the country's overall tax system. He wrote this book to provide a basic understanding of that system and a number of possible modifications that seem likely to improve the system.

www.ingramcontent.com/pod-product-compliance
Lightning Source LLC
Chambersburg PA
CBHW051727170526
45167CB00002B/836